Panther

Text by Thomas Anderson
Color plates by Vincent Wai

CONCORD
PUBLICATIONS COMPANY

ISBN 962-361-610-4
Printed in Hong Kong

Back cover photo:
This Panther is the pride of the collection at the Munster German tank museum. The vehicle is a Pzbflswg Panther (command tank) fitted with extra radio equipment. The photo was taken by kind permission of Lt.Col. Kuhlke during a celebration in 1993.

Introduction

The word "tank" is an eternal synonym for war and destruction. Hardly any other weapon affects our imagnations and fears like an armored vehicle. A lot has been written regarding tanks . . . and German tanks in particular. *Panzer* , or tank, is one of the most well-known German words in the world. *Panzers* were the ultimate weapons - the true land-takers - of the last great war. *Panzers* started the aggression in Poland and France, where they would gain the great and stunning victories of the *Blitzkrieg* era. Led by farsighted and capable officers, and manned by highly trained and motivated crews, *Panzers* would conquer large parts of Europe and menace England and the remnants of Great Britain's empire in Northern Africa. In 1941 the *Panzers* rolled into their greatest and last adventure - Operation "Barbarossa". But after a series of unbelievable victories, they would meet a superior adversary. The drive to Moscow, the siege of Leningrad, the attack of Stalingrad, and the subsequent failed campaigns of 1943, marked the turning point of WW II. The *Panzers* were stopped, repulsed and finally beaten by the *tridsatchetverka* - the famous Soviet T-34 main battle tank.

It is not the author's intention to rewrite portions of WW II's history, nor to unveil new and spectacular facts of this book's subject, the Panther MBT. This book was written for the military enthusiast. The unbiased reader who enjoys history will find interesting information on this weapon system, and the armor modeler will come to understand its evolution and the changes and improvements of its service life.

This book is a result of careful examination of many sources. Both modern and old publications were analyzed. Interviews with those who fought, suffered in and lived with the Panther tank added precious details. The author was able to talk to many veterans - rather ordinary *Panzermänner* (tankers) moreso than the *Ritterkreuzträger* (Knights of the Iron Cross). The examination of wartime files helped the author to make some interesting judgments. The photos in this book were provided in part by public archives, but more were donated by veterans and other private collectors.

The author wishes to thank veterans Helmut Berger, Erwin Bernhardt, Horst Hoppe, Paul Kammann, Werner Kriegel and Helmut Lenz for their patience and encouragement during long conversations. Special thanks go to Sergei Netrebenko of St. Petersburg (with his special interest in destroyed tanks), who researched Russian archives, and Adam Geibel, who dug through US archives and unveiled a lot of unknown documents. Thanks, too, to Michael Green, who provided precious photos of US and British vehicles. Photos were provided by Wolfgang Schneider, Karlheinz Münch, Henry Hoppe, Steven Zaloga, Frank Schulz, Heiner Duske, Franz Schmidt, Oliver Morling and Waldemar Troijca. The author used the German Bundesarchiv in Koblenz (photos credited "BA") during his research, and photos of the WW II Bilderstelle Leipzig (BL). Vincent Wai created the remarkable color plates to the complete satisfaction of the author's wishes.

The Long Way To The Panther (Operational History)

"Enemy introduced new tank! Shape roughly similar to 'Tridsatchedverka' [the T-34 , author]. Tank is heavily armored, weight is est. 40 - 50 tons. Armament is probably 88 mm AA gun. We had losses at combat ranges beyond 2,000 m. . . ."

(Radio message from 8 July 1943, sender unknown. Source: Central Armed Forces Museum, Moscow.)

This alarming radio message announced the combat debut of Germany's Panther tank. Alongside its heavier brother-in-arms, the Tiger tank, this sophisticated weapon system set new standards in armored warfare. The legendary Tiger dominated the 1943 battlefields with a certain aura of invincibility. Due to limited production numbers, this tank was primarily used at points of main effort. The Panther, however, was to be the new mass-produced German tank, intended to replace the then-obsolete Pzkw IV MBT. The reasons why the *Panzertruppen* could never do their job without the latter and why the Panther's production numbers never reached the factual neccessaries were manifold and are not the subject of this book.

July 1941 - The Challenge

In July 1941 the attack on the Soviet Union - Operation "Barbarossa" - began. This "Napoleonic" campaign was not undisputed; leading German staff officers felt that the German Army was not in the proper shape to fulfill Hitler's expectations. The front was divided into three giant military objectives: *Heeresgruppe Nord* (Army Group North) was to destroy the enemy in the Baltic, then reach and take Leningrad and all other ports; *Heeresgruppe Mitte* (Army Group Center) was to extend its wings to enclose the mainstay of the Red Army around Smolensk, and then support the northern and southern forces; and *Heeresgruppe Süd* (Army Group South) was to advance between the Pripjet swamps and the Carpatians, then seize Kiev and drive further into the industrial area of the Donets area.

The course of Operation "Barbarossa" seemed to confirm the Allies' worst expectations, and Great Britain and the US watched the situation with great concern. The Soviets could field the world's largest armored force - the number of tanks was estimated at around 18,000 - but most of these tanks were old vehicles that represented the state of the art of the early

'30s. Furthermore, a large portion of these armored vehicles were technically worn out and close to being phased out.

The German armored formations never reached their planned strength, a situation that would last over the course of the war. The inventory of the units involved amounted to 3,300 tanks, many of which were obsolete by 1941 standards. Also, the German forces were dispersed over a front longer than 1,240 miles (2,000 km). But the German aggressors' sophisticated strategy of encircling wide areas, combined with rapid tactical movements, again proved to be invincible. After some three weeks German troops had reached Smolensk, 200 miles (320 k/m) from Moscow. Thousands of enemy tanks had been destroyed or captured, and 400,000 Soviet soldiers had been captured. It is interesting that this successful start was made with comparatively weak forces.

The reasons for the Germans' initial success were manifold. Firstly, it must not be forgotten that a certain element of surprise helped the Germans. Although the Soviets were fully aware of the danger at their western borders, the German attack came as a shock, especially to the border troops. While the German troops were

highly organized, the Soviet military was weakened by Stalin's drastic purges of the late '30s, which left the Red Army with a dangerous void in its general staff. Although the Red Army's tank tactics were vastly improved during the '30s, the Soviet troops had not been fully introduced to and trained in them. The effectiveness of the German leadership principles was outstanding, and tactics were tested and further improved during the early campaigns. Wireless communication was another key of success. Every single armored vehicle was fitted with a receiver/transmitter system, thus a steady and reliable liasion was ensured.

A nasty surprise for the German troops was the appearance of the T-34, which proved to be a superior opponent for the German tanks. This tank combined firepower, protection and mobility in a degree that must be called revolutionary. Indeed, the T-34 was the first modern tank. The design featured sloped steel plates at all sides with 45 mm maximum armor (penetrating range 90 mm). The 7.62 mm tank gun was the first long-caliber gun used in a tank, and its performance was outstanding. Mobility was very good with a power/weight ratio of 18 HP/t. The 500 HP

The Panther appeared in early 1943, and this photo gives a good impression of its shape. This vehicle shows a late Ausf. D, as evidenced by the fact that the right headlamp was deleted. The muzzle brake is not yet fitted, but the gun does show a protective cover. The Panther lacks all equipment, indicating that it is brand new. The unusual license plate shows a Berlin number (1A). Since the color of the vehicle appears to be dark grey, this well known photo has often been dated from 1942. (M.Green)

Diesel engine had a lower consumption rate than comparable Otto cycle engines. Thus, speed and cruising range could be increased. An indigenous compressed air system allowed the engine to be started even in the harshest winter. Wide tracks enabled movement in worst mud. In short, the T-34 was the ideal tank for coping with Russian weather conditions.

Hitler was quoted during a conference in the Chancellery on the 29th of November, 1941 as follows:

"The experiences during the eastern campaign prove that we finally came to a turning point. Our antitank weapons are no longer effective against some of the Soviet tanks. The armor protection of our tanks is no longer sufficient against the Soviet antitank weapons . . . Since weakly armored tanks are useless, an increase in the armor protection of [our] tanks must be made even at the cost of speed."

1942 - The Last Victories

Work on the new tank began in early 1942. Daimler-Benz suggested a tank that, in its most important components, was a clear copy of the T-34. The VK 30.01 (DB) was rejected. The manufacturing firm of MAN got the production order for their design in May 1942. A mere four months later, in an outstanding technical achievement, the first two prototypes were ready. Mass-production of the Ausf. D was begun in early 1943. Development of the Panther MBT was accompanied by the last great victories in the East.

The year 1942 was a successful one for Germany´s armed forces, which gained control of a huge amount of terrain. But the essential military objectives - the invasion of the Caucasian oil fields, the shortening of the incredibly long front line reaching from Leningrad to the Black Sea, and the subsequent destruction of the Soviet armed forces - could not be achieved. The Soviets were able to direct the German summer offensive into the outskirts of their country, where it fell flat, nearly ineffective. This, however, was only possible at the price of the loss of enormous amounts of land. In the fall of 1942 the Sixth Army reached the River Volga and took Stalingrad, but the German troops were exhausted. The Soviet counterattack encircled Stalingrad around November, and at Christmas 1942 the German relief atttack was repulsed.

1943 - The Decision at the Kursk Salient

Hitler demanded the delivery of 250 Panthers for an offensive in the Kursk salient (Operation "Zitadelle"). He planned to destroy the mainstay of the Soviet Army with one large offensive, and he insisted that the new tank developments (beside the Panther MBT, the Ferdinand tank hunter and the Tiger Ausf. E heavy tank) be available in substantial numbers for this operation. This was not possible, and therefore the beginning of "Zitadelle " was postponed from the 15th of May to the 25th of June. This date proved to be impossible as well, and the attack was again put off until the 5th of July.

At dawn on the 5th, the attack began. Two giant tank battles took place north and south of Kursk. Two hundred Panthers belonging to Pz.Abt. 51 and 52 fought in the fierce struggles.

Gefreiter Werner Kriegel of Pz.Abt. 51 remembers:

"We were very nervous, since everybody put great hope in the new Panther tanks . . . We faced many problems in the days before the attack. On the 3rd of July we noticed signs of sabotage. We discovered screws in the oil reservoir of some Panthers; another had steel wool in the final drive. The Hiwis (Russian volunteers) in our camp were immidiately relieved and sent to other units. We had no losses due to these events. Our superior officers were concerned that Ivan [the Soviet Army, author] knew about our plans . . . As a driver I spent most of my spare time in the engine compartment . . . At 5 a.m. on the 5th of July we headed north towards Kursk. The Soviet defense at the Voronesh front was terrible. Our first attack stuck in a mine field. I lost a track. While our artillery suppressed the Soviets, we could recover both disabled tanks . . . The reserve companies rushed for a second attack. While we were safe at the engineer's, the first day ended in disaster. By the evening of the 5th, Pz.Abt. 51 had only 22 Panthers operational. Some 28 or so tanks were totally destroyed, the rest damaged. My comrades complained of weak final drives and of their engines overheating. The engine compartment was very tight and sealed because of the UK-equipment (diving equipment) . . . On the 8th of June we again headed for Obojan south of Kursk. Our tank received a hit from a tank gun at the commander´s cupola. We carried on the attack with an open hatch and a cracked cupola. My commander still has the shell . . . We lost one tank to one of these heavy assault guns [SU-152, author], the mantlet was simply penetrated. We also met American tanks [M3A3 Lee, author], which were no match for us . . . We destroyed a number of T-34s at ranges well over 2500 m . . ."

This report does not completely describe the seriousness of the situation. The "surprise" attack proved to be a disastrous failure. On the evening of the first day, only 40 of 200 Panthers were servicable. Direct combat losses were few; the majority of lost tanks had to be abandoned because of engine fires or transmission problems. The greatest tank battle at Prokorovka marked the turning point of "Zitadelle", and finally the war.

An officer and an engineer take a critical look at the bottom section after the tank left the pool. The drive sprocket and the track are of the early type. In September 1943 new tracks with ice cleats were introduced that offered better traction on muddy or frozen ground. (BA)

Five hundred German and more than 800 Soviet tanks fought the largest tank battle in history. On the evening of the 12th both German and Soviet forces were exhausted, but the Soviets recovered first. Between the 12th and 15th of July they made a counterattack at all fronts. The decision to call off "Zitadelle" was finally made because of the Allied landing in Sicily (Operation "Husky") on the 10th of July. From that moment the Germans were finally forced into taking the defensive.

The first combat experience of the Panther cannot be called a success. Too many "teething" troubles accompanied the new tank. It was developed in a very short time, and there was no time for thorough test or evaluations. The vehicles suffered problems with the final drives that lasted until the end of 1944. The cramped engine compartment (which was sealed as a consequence of the UK-Ausrüstung/deep wading capability) resulted in engines overheating, which destroyed the engines. This problem got worse since the cooling system was too small. As a result, some engines caught fire during combat. Another problem was the supply of combustion air to the engine. This was provided via a small circular aperture behind the engine hatch. Gefr. Kriegel again remembers an episode of September 1943:

"Our platoon moved through a pine forest. The vibrations of the heavy tanks resulted in a steady 'rain' of pine needles. After a short time, the first tank broke down, and others followed. We examined the incident. The pineneedles had fallen into the air inlets and blocked it. The respective engines had stopped almost immediately. As a stop-gap solution we welded a perforated bucket over the rear air inlet" [Note: With the introduction of the Ausf. G, a welded box was added].

The alarming news from the front led to hasty improvements, which were partly introduced during the production of the Ausf. D. A good example was the cast cupola, which improved the commander´s sight and protection. With the termination of this first production lot, Ausf. A was introduced in September 1943. This version showed many improvements. Beside internal changes, the inadequate letterbox machine gun was replaced by a ball mount (the *Kugelblende 80*). This significantly improved the handling of the bow machine gun. To keep down engine fires, two cooling pipes were attached to the left exhaust of a number of Ausf. A tanks.

Beginning in September 1943 all German tanks and assault guns were provided with the antimagnetic *Zimmerit* paste. This paste was applied on all vertical or sloped armor plates on the hull and turret. New vehicles received the coating at the factory. In the case of the Panther, some of the last Ausf. Ds, virtually all Ausf. As, and a portion of Ausf. G tanks left the production halls with *Zimmerit*. Many Ausf. Ds, however, were provided with the coating at the front, so the patterns differed widely. In September 1944 application of *Zimmerit* was ended, partly because there were rumors that *Zimmerit* had caused vehicle fires (this was disproved by tests in autumn 1944) and partly because the Soviets did not use magnetic shaped charges! So it is questionable whether the expenses were advantageous. One effect, however, cannot be denied. The enemies were impressed by the ominous coating. Major H.K. Lorance, commanding officer of 899 T.D. Battalion, notes in his evaluation report "Lessons Learned on Mk V Tanks":

"I. Camouflage: The German has outdone himself here. The tanks observed were covered with a linoleum-like surface glued to the hull and turret. This had a rippled surface to reduce glare and is painted in shades of green much as an American parachute . . . The result is as perfect a camouflage in this green hedgerow country as can be obtained . . ."

Another anecdote is told by Robert Pertuss, designing engineer of Tiger Ausf. E and Ausf. B:

"When the British finally came to Henschel [manufacturer of the Tiger] Kassel, they seemed to be more interested in this ridiculous *Zimmerit* coating than in our fine Tiger tanks . . . I was interrogated many hours about nothing but *Zimmerit*."

1944 - Retreat at all Fronts

In April 1944 production of Ausf. A commenced. The following Ausf. G showed a major redesign of the hull. The prominent wedge on the rear of the superstructure´s side was deleted, and the slope angle of the side armor plates was now steeper. To maintain armor protection, the thickness of the side walls was increased from 1.67 inches to 2 inches (40 to 50 mm). During production many further detail changes and improvements were introduced, which the author will describe by means of the photos in this book.

In 1943/1944 the Panther fought on all fronts. The crews were generally pleased with the tank. The 75 mm L/70 KWK 42 was a high performance gun. Its accuracy was very good, and its armor penetration was sufficient to destroy any enemy tank at distances of more than 2,190 yards (2,000 m). Armor protection was strong enough to face any tank at normal combat ranges. The Panther proved to be a serious problem for the Allied forces. Unlike the Tiger tank, the Panther was issued to all tank units as a standard main battle tank.

The year 1944 ended the controlled retreat battles. Beginning with the spring offensive, the Soviet forces had reached a numerical superiority that basically converted the German retreat into a series of frantic running battles. Successful

This obscure photo shows a Panther of Pz.Abt. 52 during Operation "Zitadelle". Since the power train was prone to breakdown, every opportunity was used to entrain Panther units. Note that the smoke grenade dischargers have been removed. The tanks of Pz.Abt. 52 display a roaring Panther´s head as an unofficial unit badge. (M. Green)

This Ausf. A, photographed in Italy, shows an unusually scruffy *Zimmerit* coating that was slovenly smeared over the vehicle without any rippled pattern being created. Note the ice cleats on the tracks. The gun sight is of the later monocular type. (W. Troijca)

A Panther unit as viewed over a muzzle brake. The Panthers of Panzer-Lehr Division are of various production lots. The photo was taken immidiately after the invasion of France. (F. Schulz)

counterattacks were the exception, but in August 1944 the combined forces of the IV. SS-Panzerkorps inflicted a disastrous defeat on the 2nd Belorussian tank army northeast of Warsaw.

The German forces in Italy failed to repulse the enemy despite two counterattacks. The fighting there and in the Balkan region was less dogged since the Allies knew that an end of the war could only be achieved in Germany.

The Allied invasion of Normandy on the 6th of June finally fulfilled the Soviet wish to create a second front. Up to the very last moment Hitler ignored the invasion, expecting the Western allies to attack Denmark. His personal astrologer had advised him:

"Due to the position of Saturn at the cardinal point of Cancer, I can predict an assault in northwest Europe - the Danish coast."

Hitler adopted this possibility in his order No. 51. Not impressed by this, the Allies reinforced their forces in the Normandy region. The German counterattack that was launched three days after the invasion had only limited success. On July 1 Cherbourg surrendered. American, British and Canadian forces now headed north. In August, Rennes, Le Mans and Falaise were taken. Although Panthers were the superior tanks here as well, Allied air supremacy nailed the German tank units to the ground. In fact, more tanks were lost to air raids than to ground fighting.

In November 1944 Antwerp was taken, and at the beginning of December Allied troops reached the *Westwall* - the German defensive line. In a last attempt to throw back the Western allies, the Germans launched the Ardennes offensive. Twenty-eight divisions with 250,000 men, 800 tanks and more than 300 assault guns began an assault on British and American units on the 16th of December. Bad weather favored the German troops: the Allied planes could not take off. After initial success, the attack came to a standstill on the 23rd. The very successful *Panzergruppe Peiper* was stopped when courageous American soldiers burned 132,000 gallons (500,000 liters) of fuel.

During this offensive Operation "Greif" took place, with Pz.Brig. 150, led by SS-Ob.Stbf. Skorzeny, employing heavily disguised tanks. Stug III assault guns were provided with unusual side skirts and a modified engine plate. The most interesting vehicle used in this raid was the so-called Ersatz M10, which were modified Panthers. The shapes of the hulls and turrets were disguised with sheet metal to ressemble the US M10 tank destroyer. The prominent commander´s cupola was removed, and the opening was covered by sheet metal flaps. (As a result, the commander had no proper vision.) Ten Panthers and an unknown number of Stug IIIs and APCs were thus modified. All were sprayed olive green and given US-style markings. Also, the crews wore US uniforms and carried American small arms. The purpose of this operation was to attack enemy headquarters behind the main line of resistance (MLR). Apparently this raid did not take place, and all the vehicles were destroyed in defensive combat.

1945 - The Surrender

The year 1945 saw heavy fighting around the former borders of Germany. Warsaw and Krakow were lost in January, and East Prussia was cut off. The counteroffensive to relieve Budapest failed. The intelligence department *Fremde Heere Ost* "estimated the Soviet superiority as follows: tanks 5:1; artillery 7:1; infantry 7:1. In the West another counteroffensive against the Vogesen mountains was repulsed, and the Westwall defensive line was quickly negotiated. Bonn and Koblenz fell in March, and the British headed north to invade Schleswig-Holstein. The beginning of April saw Berlin encircled. Still, the war would last for another five bloody, and senseless, weeks. Locally, *Panzer* units, especially those equipped with Panthers, achieved stunning victories. Lt. Berger of "Grossdeutschland" remembers:

"At the beginning of April, shortly before being transferred to Austria, we had a last counteroffensive at Kustrin - with a mixed combat group of six Panthers and four Pzkw IVs. On one occasion three Panthers stopped a Soviet attack under lucky conditions. Concealed at a river bank, our Panthers were able to destroy eleven T-34s, a number of assault guns [probably SU-100s, author] and about five "Stalin Panzers" [JS-IIs, author]. The Soviets were shocked, and waited another 12 hours before trying it again. Our troops, however, had already left the positions without losses."

On the 7th of May the capitulation treaty was signed - the war was over.

Order of Battle

The first units to be equipped with Panther MBTs were Pz.Abt. 51 and 52, which were sent to the Kursk salient in May/June 1943. Each battalion had about 100 Panther tanks, an exceptionally high number - but Operation "Zitadelle" was regarded as most important. On the other hand, the new tanks displayed many problems; possibly this was another reason for the generous issuance of the equipment.

A normal Panther *Abteilung* (battalion) of 1943 had a fixed strength of 76 Panthers, which were divided among four companies of 17 tanks. Eight more Panthers were in the battalion's staff company. Some lucky battalions even had reserve tanks. However, steady losses and insufficient resupply and reinforcement decreased the average strength.

It was Hitler's wish that large numbers of Panthers be sent directly to the front for immediate action, but actually the respective units were tasked to send selected battalions back to Germany to be refitted there. Far too often, however, these converted units were not returned to the struggle at the eastern front, but were kept in reserve at army command. By the end of 1943, some 1,000 of these vehicles were in service in ten *Wehrmacht Abt.* (army battalions) and in five more *Waffen-SS* or *Luftwaffe* units. By the end of 1943, Panther battalions stood ready at all fronts.

It was planned that all tank divisions would be equipped with two Panther battalions. However, the capacitiy of the German industry could never reach the aspired-to production targets. For example, in late 1944 the production output for the Panther for April 1945 was fixed at 450 units . . . but only 20 were produced! Only one battalion received Panthers; the others had to be content with Pzkw IV, assault guns or other vehicles. Regarding the theoretical "Panzerdivision 44" (a pure planning unit), these shortcomings were accepted; two tank battalions with mixed equipment was standard. The *Panzergrenadierdivision* (amored infantry division) "Kurmark" is a good example: *1. Abteilung* had three companies equipped with Hetzer tank destroyers; *2. Abteilung* had three Panther companies.

Similar to the *schwere Panzerabteilungen* (heavy tank battalions), which were equipped with Tiger Ausf. E or Ausf. B, independent *Panzerbrigaden* were organized. These units were provided with one *Panzerabteilung* only, Pz.Brig. 106 "Feldherrnhalle" being an example. This organization structure was not successful since it lacked integrated combat support and logistic units. *Panzerbrigaden*, being very flexible, were often used as *Feuerwehr* (fire brigade) units.

Towards the end of the war tank units were established with all kinds of available vehicles. Still called a division, the *Panzerdivision* "Müncheberg" was formed around 31 tanks in March 1945 - 11 Pzkw IVs (1st Co.), 10 Panthers (2nd Co.) and 10 Tiger Ausf. Es (3rd Co.).

German Combat Tactics

During the successful years of the *Blitzkrieg* era, German tank troops employed a mixture of equipment. Pz.Rgt. 25, the main tank force of *7. Panzerdivision*, reported its strength as of 12 April 1940 as follows: 37 Pzkw Is, 72 Pzkw IIs, 23 Pzkw IVs, 48 Pzkw 38(t)s. These tanks were divided into three battalions, each having two light and one heavy company.

The four different types of tanks used in one regiment gave several basic problems. In a normal attack situation, the heavy tanks had to be detached to the light companies to provide support fire with their 75 mm guns. The tactic used for this attack was brought into line with this vehicle mix. When moving, the armor

Photographed in February 1945, these late-model Panther Ausf. Gs move into defensive postions at the village of Ortwig near Küstrin. Here the Soviets had built up a bridgehead some 31 miles (50 km) east of Berlin. The Panthers show the distinctive reinforced gun mantlet. For camouflage, diagonal stripes were sprayed in broad lines over the dark yellow base color. (BA)

formation resembled a wedge, the so-called *Panzerkeil*. The light Pzkw II and 38(t) would form the point of this wedge, with orders to break through the enemy lines. The Pzkw IV (with the very thin armor it carried in1940) would form the rear flanks of the wedge. From this mobile position they monitored the battlefield, ready to put out of action enemy antitank artillery, heavy tanks and other targets. Usually this wedge attack occured in two to three waves, depending on the doggedness of resistance. When the thrust penetrated the enemy lines, the point of the wedge would spread out to chase single enemy tanks and artillery positions. The Pzkw IVs, and the Pzkw Is that followed up, would perform mopping up duties. It should be clear to the reader that the success of the German tank force depended more on these flexible tactics of concentrated tank attacks than on the fighting strength of the tanks involved.

During replenishment in France in 1942, *7. Panzerdivision* was reorganized. The number of battalions was reduced to two. Each battalion had 1 Pzkw II, 62 Pzkw IIIs (Ausf. H and L), and 13 Pzkw IVs (armed with the 75 mm L/43 tank gun) in three companies. An assault gun brigade (Stug. Abt. 232) reinforced the division with 21 Stug IIIs (75 mm L/43). The *Panzerkeil* was still the standard tactic in attack situations, with the Pzkw III forming the wedge tip and the Pzkw IV monitoring their action. However, due to the urgent cry for better tank guns that were able to deal with the masses of T-34 MBTs, the L/43-armed Pzkw IVs were often used at the point of penetration. Accordingly, the *Panzertruppe* demanded supply of more long-barrelled Pzkw IVs. With the Pzkw IV slowly but surely assuming the role of main battle tank, the concept of the heavy company became obsolete.

The fighting during the period of 1942/43 had definitively shown that the Pzkw III and IV, though both were upgunned and uparmored, were hopelessly obsolete. The Soviet doctrine to reinforce the defense lines with large numbers of antitank guns (*Pakfront*) generally stopped any attempts at a concentrated breakthrough. Soviet lines could be penetrated only by incurring heavy German losses. So Pz.Rgt. 25 reported only 5 Pzkw IVs in February 1943.

The supply of greater numbers of medium Panthers and heavy Tiger tanks resulted in newly established combat tactics. The *Panzerkeil* was replaced by the *Panzerglocke*, which resembled the shape of a bell. The wide part of the bell was

This Panther Ausf. G was destroyed in the town of Posen. It shows two penetrations at the hull front, probably from an 85 mm gun. Both shots were probably stopped by the transmission, allowing the crew to escape. As typical for late-war Panthers, the vehicle carries extra tracks and spare running wheels on the turret. The tank has been camouflaged with whitewash. (S. Netrebenko)

formed by the heavier Panther (or Tiger) tanks, which would break through the enemy lines in a frontal attack, relying on their superior armored protection., The Pzkw IIIs or IVs followed on the flanks of the bell. When enough Panthers or Tigers were available, this tactic proved to be effective. However, the times of large-scale attack operations were over by mid-1943, and the Germans were forced to go on the defensive. Attacks were now primarily made to achieve specific objectives, such as clearing up critical situations or shortening overstressed front lines.

While on the defensive, the Panther could rely on its strong points - heavy armor and a hard-hitting gun. The flexible defense on the Eastern Front cost the Soviets immense losses at a proportion of 4-5 of their own tanks for every German tank destroyed.

In the period of 1944/45 the average number of tanks per armored division was only about 30 operational vehicles. This number tended to be further reduced by direct losses and the inability to recover or repair damaged vehicles. With the days of large-scale operational *Panzerdivisions* gone, *Kampfgruppen* (battle groups), which were formed around a few tanks or assault guns, had to bear the burden of defending Germany.

Obgefr. Volkens of 2./Pz.Brig. 106 FHH remembers:

"On the 7th of March 1945 the remnants of two companies of *Feldherrnhalle* (FHH) were in Bonn. As far as I [a gunner in a Panther, author] could judge the situation, everybody was in panic. Large formations of the US 3rd Armored Division menaced our positions. In the previous fightings at the beginning of March, we lost more than two-thirds of our tanks, the rest being deployed to various *Kampfgruppen*. Our tank belonged to Kampfgruppe Böhlke (the commander of the lead tank). We had three Panthers, four SPWs with Drilling (Sd.Kfz. 251/21 with triple MG 151s) and some standard SPWs (Sd.Kfz. 251/1 APC). Standard procedure was to delay the allied advance. Teams composed of one Panther, one Drilling-SPW and two standard SPWs were placed in ambush positions. Whenever enemy infantry would advance, the 251/21 would search for them, make contact, and fight against them. The Drillings, which were intended for antiaircraft use, proved to be particularly effective in the ground defense role. If tanks were needed, our Panthers would move up. At combat ranges of less than 220 yards (200 m), every hit was a fatal one. Although we had losses, our advance was successful. The main force of FHH (what was left over) could retreat over one of the few intact Rhine River bridges. However, my family later told me that the Wehrmachtsbericht (a radio program) reported 'the heroic end of FHH', as my family later told me".

Training

By late 1942 the first two Panthers were ready for trials, which took place at the Berka training area. Large-scale production of the new tank, to begin in the spring of 1943, was subsequently ordered. By June some 170 Panthers had been delivered.

Beginning with production of the tanks, the *Panzertruppenschule* (armor school) was ordered to organize instruction courses for the Panther. The commander of 1./Pz.Lehr.Rgt. started the first course in Erlangen. The proximity to the manufacturer (MAN) in Nuremberg and the large shooting range of Grafenwöhr allowed for an intensive industrial care and good training possibilities. Until the end of the war, Erlangen instructed all officers, platoon leaders, driving instructors, and all engineer personnel for the Panther units of the *Wehrmacht* and *Waffen-SS*.

The first units to be equipped with Panthers were Pz.Abt. 51 (the former Austrian Pz.Rgt. 33) and Pz.Abt. 52. Shortly after establishment in Mailly-le-Camp (France), crews and officers trained on the new weapon system at the Grafenwöhr training area. This training took place during the period of anticipation prior to the upcoming Operation "Zitadelle", and due to intense time pressure, the quality of training suffered. In particular, it was not possible to sufficiently practice the much-improved tactical mobility of the Panther. The Panthers of Grafenwöhr still presented severe problems, but since these vehicles were already in service for some weeks, the school mechanics learned how to deal with them. The resultant catastrophe would occur near Kursk.

Gefreiter (private) Werner Kriegel remembers:

"I was ordered to Grafenwöhr to join 1./Pz.Abt. 51 in March 1943. Here I started my driving school training, which would last for eight weeks. I remember a company roll-call when we received very strict orders. We were not allowed to take private photos of the Panther and were instructed not to speak of it in the public. Furthermore, there were no written notes allowed; we were ordered to commit everything to memory . . . It was rather amusing that even our instructors were helpless far too often, since even they had no notes... I always considered my basic training on the Panther as effective . . . We youngsters felt very proud that we got the new tanks, and not the old and experienced

tankers . . . The driving school vehicles were different from later Panthers in some aspects . . :"

The interview with Mr. Kriegel revealed that the driving school vehicles of 1./Pz.Abt. 51 displayed a number of specific features. Basically identical to later Ausf. D Panthers, some *Fahrschul-Panther* had the early single baffle muzzle brake as used with the Pzkw IV/F2. All vehicles [Mr. Kriegel remembers 4 to 6] were prepared for deep wading/diving. Externally, a large horizontal exhaust with a snorkel valve was fitted at the rear plate. A flat dome covered the air inlet on the engine cover. This dome contained a telescopic snorkel, which could be erected to between 9 and 13 feet (3 to 4 m). According to Mr. Kriegel´s memories, all hatches were provided with special rubber sealings.

Mr. Kriegel recalls further:

"Although the *UK-Ausrüstung* [for underwater combat equipment] was shown to us, we never practiced deep wading or diving. Our instructor told us that there simply was no time as the *Abteilung* would soon be going to Russia . . . Later, in the Kursk salient, we would discover dangerous problems related to this equipment."

Non-commissioned officers were trained in the *Feld-Unteroffiziers-Schule* in Rembertow near Warsaw. Training in occupied Poland was difficult and depressing. No soldier was allowed to leave the school without an armed guard. After the collapse of Army Group Center in the summer of 1944, the unit was evacuated to the training area at Wischau, where courses carried on for another six months.

Then, after again being evacuated, this time to a village near the western border of Germany, the *F.Uffz.Sch.* fought against American troops with a mixed company of Pzkw IIIs, IVs and Panthers.

The tank school courses were primarily intended for non-commissioned officers and officers. The rank and file were transferred from various units to those equipped with Panther MBTs. Mr. Erwin Bernhardt of Pz.Rgt. 24 remembers:

" I volunteered for the *Panzertruppe* in 1941 and received basic training at 6./Pz.Ers.Abt. 1 in Erfurt. After passing the driving school (Pzkw IV), I was trained as a tank mechanic because of my civil job . . . When Pz.Rgt. 24 was newly established, I enlisted as a *Panzerwart* [tank mechanic] . . . We constantly received new men, who were trained in the tanks directly . . . "

The *Panzertruppenschulen*, established from 1934 onwards, performed well during the war. Beside Erlangen and Rembertow, there were further school garrisons in Bergen, Krampnitz, Mielau (tank hunter), Paderborn (Tiger), Putlos (shooting range), Weimar, Wünsdorf, Zossen, Paris and Versailles. Towards the end of the war, many units had to supply their badly worn vehicles for combat and defend the Reich. The author quotes a Major Rettemeier, commander of Pz.Trp.Sch. Erlangen:

"At the end of March [1945, author], we were ordered to leave the school (with all units that were fit to fight) to join Kampfgruppe "Oberst von Massenbach". The combat group fought around Würzburg between the rivers Main and Danube until they were wiped out."

Russian children playing on an abandoned Panther Ausf.D of Pz.Abt. 52. Number "735" is in excellent condition, proving that it was lost to minor damage. The driver's visor is half opened. Although this hatch provided the driver with a good view, it weakened the front armor protection. Note that the reloading/communication hatch is also open. (S. Netrebenko)

Panther Ausf. D

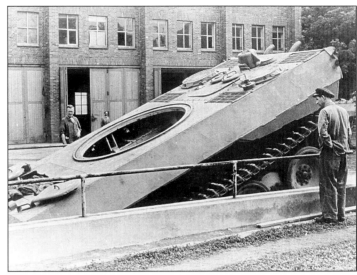

This Panther hull is being driven into a pool to check its watertightness. The dome behind the engine hatch covered the telescoping snorkel, which was intended for use during deep wading. The *Antennenfuß 1* antenna mount is visible on the engine deck. Since this early Ausf. D still lacks the gun rest used during travel that is normally fitted above the front ventilator, as well as all other equipment, it could be a prototype that was photographed during evaluations. (BA)

After being driven into the pool, the engine compartment undergoes an examination by mechanics and engineers. The dome has been removed, and the air intake (with its mesh screen) is now visible. The rear plate is bare except for the early exhaust pipe system. For deep wading, these pipes would have been replaced by a horizontally fitted muffler with a valve. (BA)

Panther Ausf. Ds wait to be shipped to their units. This photo was taken in April or May 1943, prior to the Kursk offensive. Since no Panther of this train was apparently provided with towing cables, a crew member holds a non-standard cable; he's probably waiting for a towing vehicle. A lot of wooden beams are stored on the engine deck; these were used for leverage in wedging the Panther onto the flatbed wagons. (M. Green)

The following pictures show a Panther Ausf. D at Grafenwöhr training area in April 1943. This is one of the vehicles directly issued to Pz.Abt. 51; this is no driving school tank. Of special interest is the large box on the right side of the superstructure containing the track tools. This was only provided to the first batch of vehicles. The number "135" in plain white is just visible behind the smoke grenade discharger. (W. Kriegel)

This photo gives a good impression of the Panther's size. Compared to other tanks, the Panther had a very high silhouette, making it difficult to conceal the vehicle. This overexposed photo clearly shows the brightness of the dark yellow body color. (W. Kriegel)

Proud Gefr. Kriegel standing in front of his tank, which is finished in plain dark yellow. Every feature of the early Ausf. D production is evident: the letterbox MG port, two headlights, smoke grenade dischargers, and the early commander's cupola. (W. Kriegel)

Pz.Rgt. 24 was established in 1943. After one year of hard fighting, it was sent to France for refitting. This photo was taken shortly after the invasion at a training area at Voussiers. This particular vehicle shows a mid-production Ausf. D. The commander's cupola shows an MG ring. The smoke grenade dischargers were already deleted. What makes this Panther interesting is the pyrotechnical gunfire simulator fitted onto the barrel just behind the travel rest. (E. Bernhardt)

The same vehicle from a distance. In front of it an archaic vehicle, a Pzkw II Ausf. B, can be seen. Oldtimers like this were used for tank school driving purposes up to the end of the war. The tanks of Pz.Rgt. 24 received their *Zimmerit* coating at field workshops in September/October 1943, resulting in a scruffy and uneven pattern. (E. Bernhardt)

This shows 3rd Squadron of 1./Pz.Rgt. 24 during live fire training. The gunfire simulators have been removed. The vehicle in the foreground is a late Ausf. D, as shown by the late-style commander's cupola. (E. Bernhardt)

The live firing practice is being inspected by the commanding general of *Panzergruppe West*, General Eberbach (in leather overcoat), who observes the hits with two adjudants. The *Zimmerit* on this particular vehicle appears to have been applied very hastily as not all parts of the hull were covered. (E. Bernhardt)

One-ton half-tracks provided the Panther tanks with new ammuniton. Results of the live firing were discussed with officers of the 3rd Squadron. During training the Panthers had their side skirts removed to avoid unneccessary losses. (E. Bernhardt)

Panthers were often shown in propaganda media. Here an early Ausf. D shows its superiority to an M4A1 named "War Daddy II" at a slope. Demonstrations like this were widely use to distract attention from the catastrophic situation that existed on all fronts. The text says: "General Sherman fell back. His German opponent, a new heavy tank, succeeds where the Yankee failed". (BL)

This mid-production Panther Ausf. D was provided with an improvised ladder to make it easier to mount the large tank. The *Zimmerit* coating was applied in a more precise way. Note the MG ring on the cupola. (F. Schulz)

The rear view of the same tank shows two boxes mounted on the engine compartment. In order to keep from blocking the cooling system, the boxes were carried on raised platforms. The exhaust pipes show the bright color of annealed metal. The Panther's exhaust reached very high temperatures, and the pipes often glowed. The jack is still mounted below the cast exhaust covers. (F. Schulz)

Panther number "232" is seen here speeding on its way. The crew has added a support for the swiveling commander's hatch. (The swivel hinge occasionally warped during rough driving.) Note that *Zimmerit* has even been applied to the side skirts. The crew's five steel helmets are stored outside the vehicle. (F. Schulz)

This early Panther Ausf. D shows no *Zimmerit*. Apparently, its crew added a ladder and supply crates. The vehicle is painted in an elaborately applied three-tone camouflage scheme. In 1943 this job was done by the troops, who could choose the scheme that was best suited to the respective vegetation or season. (K. Münch)

Panther "632" negotiates a slope. These situations could become serious, as the bottom of the tank featured only weak armor. Additionally, enemy shells would hit the plates at 0 degrees, making penetration very likely. This tank was converted to a mobile veranda by adding what looks to be quite a comfortable bench. (K. Münch)

Panthers assemble after combat. Again, these are early Ausf. Ds, as is evident by the smoke grenade dischargers. Certain parts of the equipment are missing, though. The shackles were probably already installed for easy recovery. A group of captured Soviet soldiers wait in front of one tank to be transported to a POW camp. (K. Münch)

The same unit waiting for enemy contact. Behind the Panther Ausf. D (early production lot) is hidden a Pzbflswg III. A lot of these older command tanks were used with Panther units. Though they were prime targets for the enemy, the one in the background seems to be intact. (K. Münch)

A late-model Ausf. D in or near Uman, Russia in early 1944. The tank lacks the right headlamp and is provided with the cast commander's cupola. Ice cleats have been added to the tracks. To the right of the gun barrel are visible the two openings for the early binocular tank sight. This photo gives a good example of the problems the muddy seasons created for the German transport units. The Panther is ready to tow a disabled vehicle. (K. Münch)

Tanks of 5.SS-Pz.Div. "Wiking" prior to combat near Kovel in April/May 1944. This unit played an important part in breaking through the pocket around that city. Both vehicles, late Ausf. Ds, show partly damaged *Zimmerit* coatings. The camouflage consisted of narrow stripes of dark green and brown over the dark yellow base, which were probably applied with brushes. The Panther at right shows a 6.5-ft (2 m) rod antenna fitted on its roof and a 4.5-ft (1.4 m) rod antenna on the standard mount behind the turret. That means this could be a *Flivo* tank (Sd.Kfz. 268 ground-to-air liaision vehicle). (W. Schneider)

Back at Kovel Panther "501" of 5.SS-Pz.Div. is seen moving toward an enemy postion. The white numbers are clearly evident. German tanks showed a wide variety of tactical markings like this. The commander looks carefully out of his hatch, his headphone leaving one ear free to listen to combat noise. The rear hatch was opened to improve ventilation. (W. Schneider)

Moving on to France now, we see a late Ausf. D of Panzer-Lehr Division waiting for action. The early Panthers had a binocular tank sight, as is indicated by the two apertures to the right of the gun. *Zimmerit* on this tank is of the "handmade" style that was added by front line troops. Note that even the mud guards have been smeared over with it. (F. Schulz)

A Panther Ausf. D (late model) of 8.Company moves up in an effort to offer cover for a *Panzergenadier* (armored infantry) squad - elements of the armored infantry. The fighting around Kovel inflicted heavy losses on both German and Soviet forces. The camouflage on this vehicle has been applied with an airbrush. (W. Schneider)

Advancing slowly to the MLR (main line of resistance), early Ausf. D Panthers of "Grossdeutschland" prepare for a battle at the eastern border of Rumania. Soviet forces tried to take Targul-Frumos, an important junction, but their attacks failed several times. Some 250 tanks were destroyed by "Grossdeutschland", among them many JS-II heavy tanks. In this situation, the Panthers were able to take full advantage of their excellent 75 mm KWK L/70 guns. (W. Troijca)

A Panther Ausf. D (early production) lies abandoned in a Russian village. The vehicle is probably part of Pz.Abt. 51. No destructive hit is visible, so it is likely that it suffered a mechanical breakdown, as many others did. The gun mantlet shows a hit that slipped off. A smaller dent, which is visible at the cupola, is probably the result of an antitank rifle. A strange Stug III Ausf. G is visible in the background. The gun assembly has been removed, and the opening closed with a box-like structure. A modified vehicle like this could have been used as a recovery vehicle or, judging by the round apertures, an artillery forward observer. (S. Netrebenko)

This view of a demolished Panther Ausf. D shows details of the tank's rear plate. The jack is missing, and the fittings over the circular maintenance plate are open. The small tube under the left storage box is the late-style rear light (distance indicator). The vehicle carries two extra roadwheels, as the early 16-bolt wheels were prone to breaking. As with all vehicles used during Operation "Zitadelle", *Zimmerit* was not applied. (S. Netrebenko)

The rear of the same Panther shows the deep-wading dome on the air inlet. This could be proof that Pz.Abt. 51 and/or 52 still had this equipment at the baggage train. The smoke grenade dischargers, however, are missing. Camouflage probably consisted of dark green blotches over dark yellow. (S. Netrebenko)

Panther number "633", an early Ausf. D of Pz.Abt. 52, was destroyed during Operation "Zitadelle". Note the pistol port cover hanging at its chain, which was possibly blown out by an internal explosion. Also, the armor skirt supports are visible. This arrangement was quite prone to damage, and many Panthers lost their skirts during combat. The crews often fixed additional brackets for them. A Panther head insignia is barely visible in front of the turret number. (S. Netrebenko)

Crew members perform maintenance on the track of a Panther Ausf. D (late production). They are exchanging the track pins, which is the weakest point of any running gear. Since the Panther is fitted with a monocular gunsight and the loader's periscope, this could very well be an early Ausf. A. This photo was taken in early 1944 so the tank's whitewash is still just visible. The unit symbol on the glacis plate is unknown. Note the machine gun mounted on the commander's cupola. (W. Schneider)

This photo shows the impressive shape of the Panther MBT. This late Ausf. D (binocular gun sight) is covered with a factory-applied *Zimmerit* coating. The turret number, "833", was handpainted in white. Note that the front sections of the side skirts and parts of the mudguards are missing. (W. Schneider)

Panthers of 5.Company (probably of "Wiking") assemble at a factory yard. The first vehicle, which is probably an Ausf. D, illustrates the original horizontal position of the jack. The next Panther is an Ausf. A, as is evident by the vertical jack and the cooling pipes attached to the left exhaust. The tanks display a very scruffy camouflage of dark brown and dark green stripes. Covered in mud and dust as all of them are, the tanks blend in perfectly with their surroundings. (W. Schneider)

The late-model Ausf. D at right shows remnants of winter whitewash on its turret and hull. Of interest is the gun, which has apparently been replaced recently. The color of the Panther appears to be dark gray or green. The second vehicle, number "500", is the company leader's tank. (W. Schneider)

A Soviet infantry squad passes by a destroyed Panther Ausf. D (late production). Both the communication port and the smoke grenade dischargers were deleted during production. The tank is fitted with the later cast commander's cupola. Since all hatches are open, the crew probably managed to escape. (S. Netrebenko)

Panther "428" was painted over with whitewash. The large numbers on the side of the turret and the smaller one at the rear were painted very crudely in red. An iron cross is visible between the exhaust tubes. The *Zimmerit* was probably applied by a field workshop. Note that both track tension ports are opened, and the tension tool is still fitted in the left one.(S. Netrebenko)

Soviet soldiers inspect a Panther Ausf. D. This early production was possibly destroyed by a mine. (S. Netrebenko)

This early Panther Ausf. D was lost during "Zitadelle" as well. Two side skirts have fallen off, completely destroying their brackets. (S. Netrebenko)

Soviet Navy officers inspect a broken down Panther. The photo was probably taken in the southern districts, as is evident by the palatial houses. (S. Netrebenko)

Destroyed by a well-aimed shot that penetrated the turret, this early Ausf. D was abandoned at a farmhouse. The bracket for the smoke grenade discharger is still visible. The MG port and driver's hatch are open. (S. Netrebenko)

This convoy was destroyed either by an air raid or concentrated artillery fire. A number of trucks have virtually disintegrated. Visible in the background is an Sd.Kfz. 263 communications vehicle. (S. Netrebenko)

Another group of mangled Panthers clutter up a street. In wintertime, tanks were camouflaged by all means available - white paint, lime whitewash, and even chalk. (S. Netrebenko)

A Panther Ausf. D is loaded onto a flatbed wagon. The crew will soon wedge the tracks. During railway transport, all side skirts were removed. The tank shows a very rough coating of *Zimmerit* that is typical of early Panthers. (M. Green)

This Panther Ausf. D of "Wiking" carries a pair of double running wheels on the engine deck. These were used in the center of the interleafed running gear. The turret number is painted in plain black. (P. Kammann)

Panther "331" is being inspected by American troops. The Panther was regarded by all Allies as an excellent tank and a dangerous foe. (A. Geibel)

Panther Ausf. A

In September 1943 the second production version of the Panther, the Ausf. A, appeared on the scene. The simple letterbox MG port was replaced by the more sophisticated ball mount (*Kugelblende 80*), and the cast commander's cupola became standard. This particular Panther of 5.SS-Pz.Div. "Wiking" is already fitted with the monocular gun sight. As with most Ausf. As, it features a factory-applied *Zimmerit* coating. The vehicle is camouflaged with broad brown and green stripes over a dark yellow base. (W. Schneider)

This photo shows the impact of enemy fire on a Panther Ausf. A. The turret was penetrated by three (visible) rounds, probably of 7.62 cm caliber. Large portions of *Zimmerit* have fallen off. The roof plate over the transmission was blown off by an internal explosion. Beginning with Ausf. A, the loader was provided with a periscope. The square block welded behind the gun mantlet limited elevation of the gun. (W. Schneider)

The gun mantlet of the same tank was penetrated as well. The pattern of the *Zimmerit* coating is shown to advantage here. Note that the monocular gun sight is still provided with the wide rain cover used with the earlier binocular gun sight. (W. Schneider)

Some heavily camouflaged Panthers search for cover in a village. The closest tank shows a good deal of extra equipment. The precise version of the tank cannot be identified. (M. Green)

A platoon of Panther Ausf. As of "Wiking" moves to the front. The Panther in the foreground is fitted with ventilation pipes at the left exhaust. The jack is fitted between the exhaust tubes. Note the loader sitting in the rear hatch. (W. Schneider)

This most interesting photo shows some Panthers of "Wiking"'s *2.Abteilung*. They are unusual for several reasons. The camouflage was applied with a brush, resulting in hard-edged blotches of brown over a dark yellow base. The vehicle number of the Panther in the foreground, "II 011", probably indicates that this was a reserve vehicle of the 2nd Battalion staff. (W. Schneider)

Preparing for action! A 75 mm Pak 40 and a VW *Schwimmwagen* pass by a Panther Ausf. A as two motorcyclists take in the scenery. Tank number "II 11" belonged to the 2nd Battalion of "Wiking". (W. Schneider)

"II 02", another of 2nd Battalion's Panthers, is painted in the common camouflage scheme of green and brown stripes sprayed irregularly over the dark yellow base. This staff company vehicle was not fitted with extended radio equipment. (W. Schneider)

Panther "II 11" passes by a battered Ausf. A. Visible below the driver's hatch is a large dent, which doubtless caused some interior problems. However, the tank remained unharmed by this direct hit from a 76.2 mm gun, though some torsion bars on the left side might be broken. It is noteworthy that the complete *Zimmerit* coating on the glacis plate fell off as a result of the impact of the shell. It is possible that the tank's crew was waiting nearby for recovery. (W. Schneider)

This Ausf. A of "Wiking"'s 8.Company (2nd Battalion) also features a glacis plate that is devoid of *Zimmerit*. (Perhaps small arms fire shot it away?) The passing VW *Schwimmwagen* provides a comparison by which we can get an impression of the large bulk of the Panther. (W. Schneider)

This Panther Ausf. A was finished in the more common three-tone camouflage of brown and green stripes over a dark yellow base. The number "304" was painted in red with white outlines. (P. Kammann)

Panthers of "Wiking" are seen moving through a small wood. This Ausf. A also shows the ventilation pipes fitted to the left exhaust. (P. Kammann)

This transport train was hit either by artillery fire or an air strike. The Panther Ausf. A shows another variation of the exhaust system, with both pipes being fitted with a metal cover. The turret is provided with extra track links for added protection. Note that the number "191" was painted on the commander's cupola. The tank has been concealed by foliage. (S. Netrebenko)

An officer takes a ride on Panther number "325", another tank belonging to "Wiking". (P. Kammann)

A Panther Ausf. A of "Panzer-Lehr". Apparently this unit had not endured any severe air strikes up to the time of this photo since no foliage was applied to the tanks. Because their own fighter-bombers were not available, the Germans suffered very heavy tank losses. (F. Schulz)

This Ausf. A Panther offers a good view on its factory-applied *Zimmerit*. Note that the gun's travel rest is folded away, and the name "Gerda" is written on the mount. (F. Schulz)

This soldier has found a comfortable accomodation under a destroyed Panther. Digging holes under tanks was a common practice since such places were relatively secure against artillery strikes. (P. Kammann)

A late-model Panther Ausf. D follows an Ausf. A into a French town. The nearer vehicle is in marching order, its gun being fastened in the travel rest. A protective cover has also been pulled over the muzzle brake. (F. Schulz)

This bush is an APC! The crew of the Sd.Kfz. 250/10 (yes, this is evident by the wheels) did a good job of concealing their vehicle. The only visible crew member holds his hand on the 37 mm Pak 36. (F. Schulz)

Tankers of "Panzer-Lehr" gather for a briefing. The Panther in the background is an Ausf. A, as is indicated by the monocular gun sight. (F. Schulz)

The results of carpet bombing around a French town. Though effective, this manner of liberation was not popular with the local residents. Nevertheless, it did put this Panther Ausf. A out of action. (A. Geibel)

This Ausf. A, a very early production vehicle, is still fitted with the binocular gun sight. The bow MG is protected by a muzzle cover. The tankers wear "*Schiffchen*" field caps. Note the rough texture of the *Zimmerit* coating. (F. Schulz)

This interesting photo shows the unloading of a Panther Ausf. A at a harbor, possibly near Aberdeen Proving Ground. Being a soundly designed tank, many Panthers were evaluated by the Allies. (A. Geibel)

Destroyed by a round fired into its weak 1.7-inch (45 mm) side armor, this Panther lies abandoned in a French field. The turret's armor was reinforced by extra track links. (A. Geibel)

Soviet troops pass by a disabled Panther Ausf. A. The turret number, "124", was painted on twice, probably due to a whitewash scheme applied in the winter of 1944/45. The vehicle is in a rather good condition. (S. Netrebenko)

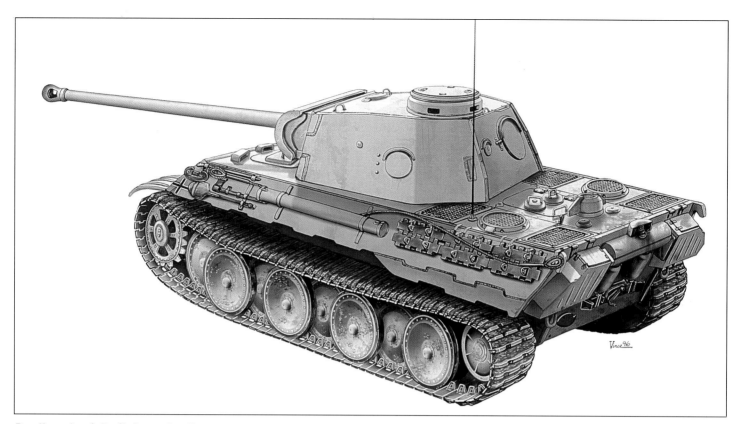

Panther Ausf. D, first production version, Grafenwöhr, spring 1943

This early Panther Ausf. D represents a training vehicle at Grafenwöhr exercise area. It belonged to the first production lot, which was used entirely for driving school purposes. According to veteran tankers, some vehicles were prepared for diving/deep wading, thus they exhibited a horizontally fitted exhaust muffler with a one-way valve. The dome on the air inlet behind the engine hatch contained a telescopic snorkel, which could be erected to a 10-13 ft (3-4 m) height. All hatches were sealed, and watertight covers could be slipped over the muzzle brake, commander's cupola and gun mantlet. Apparently, a few vehicles were provided with the single baffle muzzle brake as used with the Pzkw IV Ausf. F2.

Panther Ausf. D, early version, 1./Pz. Abt. 52, Kursk salient, summer 1943

Pz.Abt. 52 and 51 were the first units to be equipped with Panther Ausf. D MBTs. These early production vehicles had a large tool box on the right side of the hull that contained the track tools. At this point of time side skirts were not fitted, and the famous *Zimmerit* coating was not yet used. Typical for early Panthers were the cylindrical commander's cupola and the smoke grenade racks on both sides of the turret. Of special interest is the unofficial unit insignia of Pz.Abt. 52 - a roaring Panther's head.

Panther Ausf. D, middle version, Pz.Rgt. 24, Voussiers, France, autumn 1944

Pz.Rgt. 24 used a number of Ausf. Ds during basic training in Voussiers near Reims in 1944. These vehicles were standard Ausf. Ds with the early commander's cupola. During production, AA MG rings were introduced. Of great interest is the pyrotechnical gunfire simulator, which was fitted to the gun just in front of the mantlet. The Panthers produced before August 1943 had no *Zimmerit* ; this was applied by field workshops by official order. This, however, resulted in a very rough coating that was not comparable to that applied by the factory.

Panther Ausf. D , winter wash, winter 1943/44

This late-model Ausf. D. shows the newly introduced commander's cupola, which offered improved sight and protection. The large reloading/communication hatch was no longer provided. The vehicle shows no *Zimmerit*, and its equipment is standard. The tank is whitewashed, so only small portions of the base color are visible. This particular tank displayed a German iron cross at the rear plate between the exhaust pipes.

Pzkw V Panther Ausf. A, 5.SS-Pz.Div. "Wiking", Kovel, March 1944

This standard Panther Ausf. A is interesting for a couple of reasons. The camouflage scheme is unusual; it was applied by the crew with brushes. Also, a very large number is evident on the turret. Panther "II 011" is possibly a reserve vehicle for the staff of 2nd Battalion.

Pzbflswg Panther Ausf. A, 5.SS-Pz.Div. "Wiking", east of Warsaw, August 1944

This Pzbflswg Panther Ausf. A. was the vehicle of SS-Staf. Mühlenkamp, commander of 5.SS-Panzerdivision. Used as a Sd.Kfz. 267, it was provided with a star antenna located in the middle of the engine deck and a second 6.5 ft (2 m) rod antenna on the turret roof. Below the gun cleaning kit is visible a rack with three elongation pipes for the star antenna. *Zimmerit* was applied by the factory.

Pzkw Panther Ausf. G, splinter camouflage, Poland, autumn 1944

This Ausf. G shows a lot of extra equipment. The mantlet has a reinforced lower edge called a chin mantlet. This was introduced to prevent rounds from penetrating the driver´s roof. Turret protection was further enhanced by adding spare track links. The vehicle number was painted directly onto the links. Of special interest is the sharp-edged camouflage that was applied with stencils, probably by the crew.

Panther Ausf. G (0-series), Pz.Rgt. 24, near Aachen, November 1944

This vehicle is one of the few Panthers fitted with rubber-saving steel-rimmed running wheels. Apart from the running wheels, this is a standard Ausf. G. In late 1944 the camouflage scheme changed. As the front lines reached the German borders, the base color of dark yellow proved to be too bright, so the camouflage colors of dark green and dark brown were expanded to cover wider areas. Large portions of the running gear were camouflaged, which left a smaller amount of dark yellow visible.

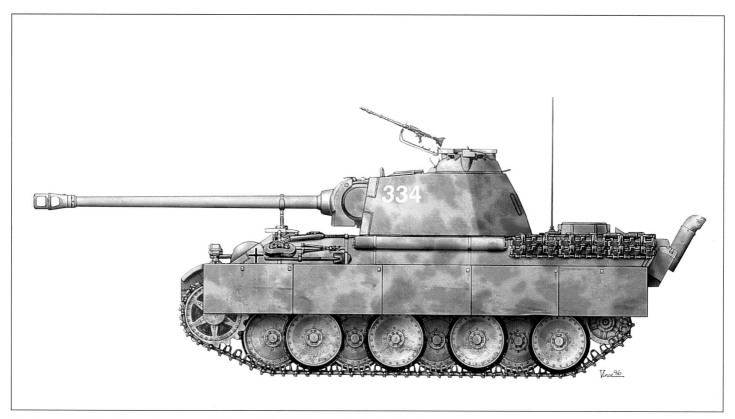

Panther Ausf. G, Kampfgruppe Pz.Brig. 106 FHH, Bonn, March 1945

This vehicle represents a very late version of the Ausf. G. All side skirts are fitted and the mantlet shows the reinforced chin. *Flammenvernichter* exhaust mufflers, which were designed to prevent the exhaust from glowing, have been fitted. (In some cases, Soviet tankers used to aim at the exhausts at night.) These also prevented backfires. (Panthers occasionally caught fire from exhaust problems.) The numbers on the turret were small, thereby creating somewhat of a low-visibility marking.

Panther Ausf. G with IR equipment (Solution A), 3./Pz.Rgt. 24, Fallingbostel, December 1944

An unknown number of Panthers of 3rd Squadron, 1st Battalion, 24th Tank Regiment were provided with infrared equipment in December 1944. This set consisted of an IR searchlight with an image converter mounted inside the commander's cupola. This simple set made possible successful combat at night. One vehicle was sent to Stuhlweißenburg, where it was tested with "Wiking". Although successful, widespread use was still delayed for some unknown reason. The base vehicle was a standard Ausf. G with the *Flammenvernichter* flame trap exhaust.

Panther Ausf. D with IR equipment (Solution B), unit unknown
This elaborate conversion provided driver, gunner and commander with a complete IR set (IR search light and image converter), which could be added without major changes to the basic MBT´s design. Although simple and prone to mechanical breakdowns, this was the first tank with full IR night-fighting capability. Precise combat reports are lacking, but all tests were successful.

Ersatz M10, Panther Ausf. G disguised as M10 TD, Pz.Brig. 150, La Falize, 1944/45
Pz.Brig.150 converted about 10 Panther Ausf. Gs to imitations of the US M10 tank destroyer. Sheet metal was used to disguise the shape of the turret and hull. Even the commander´s cupola was removed, leaving the commander without proper sight in combat. These ersatz (substitute) M10s failed during combat due to unsuitable tactics: the vehicles were sent out on normal assaults rather than being used for commando raids.

Panther Ausf. G, used by Soviet units

Many German tanks were used by Soviet units, among them a number of Panthers. These vehicles were repainted in Soviet-style dark green, then tactical markings were added. The large white star, unusual for Soviet tanks, would help to avoid misidentification. Very large white three-digit numbers were also applied.

Pzbeobwg Panther Ausf. D (artillery observer´s tank)

This artillery observer´s vehicle was a highly specialized tank. Although no combat photo of the vehicle is known to exist, several sources speak of about 50 of them being produced. The main gun was replaced by a short dummy gun. A rangefinder was mounted inside the turret, and sight was provided via two flaps on the front. Further, an observation periscope was mounted on the roof of the turret. These vehicles were provided with extended radio equipment similar to the Pzbflswg Panther Command tank.

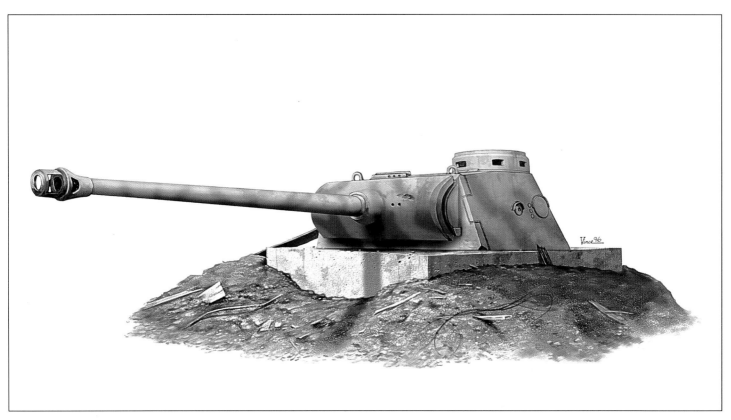

Panther turret in improvised defensive position, Berlin, 1945

This turret was one of many used in fixed positions to protect strongpoints or cities. Normally such turrets were taken from destroyed vehicles that were beyond repair. This particular turret is one of a dozen which would defend the city of Berlin against the advancing Soviet troops.

Bergepanther Ausf. G, unit unknown

The Bergepanther was probably the best recovery vehicle of WW II. It was provided with a powerful winch and a rear spade, and a crane could be erected to exchange engines or transmissions. A lot of recovery equipment and additional tools were carried by these versatile vehicles. This particular Bergepanther shows an AA MG fitted on the front.

Panther Ausf. G

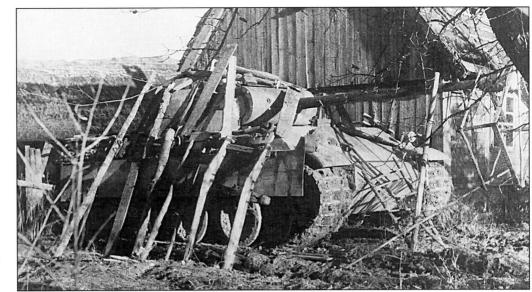

This Panther Ausf. G has been thoroughly concealed in anticipation of a Soviet attack. The wooden planks that were leaned against the tank would fall off when the tank moved. This Ausf. G was produced after September 1944, as is indicated by the lack of a *Zimmerit* coating. The larger side skirts are clearly visible. (BA)

Defending the East Prussian town of Goldap in early 1945, this Panther clearly displays the revised side plates of the Ausf. G. Due to production of the Jagdpanther, the hull's side angle was changed and the armor increased to nearly 2 inches (50 mm). The camouflage was called *Licht und Schatten Tarnung*, more commonly known as the ambush scheme. The number "213" was applied in white. (BA)

Cooperation between armored infantry and tanks was practiced as often as possible. This Waffen-SS unit takes up a position in trenches, supervised by Panther Ausf. G number "411". It displays a camouflage pattern of broad diagonal stripes of brown and green, which leaves little of the dark yellow base color visible. (BA)

After the Allied invasion could not be stopped, German tank forces in France had to be reorganized. Air raids were a constant threat, and tanks were concealed with foliage to a far greater extent than at the Eastern Front. Here *Panzergrenadiers* take a ride on a well-camouflaged Panther Ausf. G. (BA)

A Panther Ausf. G being unloaded at a port in the Baltics. Scenes like this were common in late 1944 when East Prussia was cut up by heavy attacks by the Red Army. Parts of the German civil population were evacuated over the Baltic region, but many more had to choose the dangerous route over the frozen sea. (H. Duske)

Maintenance was, and still is, one of the regular duties of tankers. The crew of this Panther is doing this job in the field. This early Ausf. G shows a very neat application of *Zimmerit*. (BA)

These tanks were photographed shortly after sea transport at Memel (11 December 1944). All Panthers show a great amount of equipment and spare tracks directly on the tanks. As Memel was isolated, a proper flow of supplies was not possible. The Lithuanian harbor city was taken by Soviet troops on 27 January 1945. (BA)

On the 15 January 1945, the Soviets launched a major assault on East Prussia. These Panthers are assembling for a counterattack. Winter whitewashed Panther "411" shows a lot of extra equipment, typical for the last months of the war. If the crews were resupplied, the vehicles would carry as much as they could hold. Two extra running wheels are fitted to the turret. In the background is visible a Bergepanther recovery vehicle. (BA)

An interesting photo showing the command post of a battlegroup. While a Pz IV/70 (V) command vehicle stands near a farmhouse, two Panther Ausf. Gs supervise the terrain back to back. All vehicles are covered with a neat winter camouflage. (Ebenrode, East Prussia, 17.01.1945). (BA)

In the spring of 1945 the eastern parts of Germany could turn into muddy swamps. This Panther Ausf. G is in a dangerous position as it negotiates a water hole. Should the tank bog down, a recovery would be impossible. (BA)

The crew of this Panther poses for a photo. This is an early Ausf. G, as the *Zimmerit* coating shows. The MG ball mount is shut up with a plug plate. (P. Kammann)

Two Panthers fire at Soviet positions in late 1944. Both vehicles are in perfect condition, with all side skirts fitted. The vehicle numbers, which are extraordinary large, cover the complete rear of the turret. (BA)

A Panther waiting for action in a French town. The hatch on the driver's side was deleted with the advent of the Ausf. G. The vehicle lacks all side skirts but carries extra track links for additional turret protection. (P. Kammann)

In early November 1944 Pz.Rgt. 24 lay in defensive postions on the German border near the city of Aachen. The era of large-scale operations was gone, and it was now up to hastily established battle groups to try to slow the Allied advance. This Ausf. G waits well-concealed in an oak forest. Note the protective cover on the muzzle brake. (E. Bernhardt)

As the commander of this early Panther Ausf. G scans the terrain carefully from his cupola, he steers the tank off the road to search for cover in the shadow of some trees. The tank's last two side skirts are missing (something that happened rather often). The rear hatch was held open for better ventilation. (F. Schulz)

A column of Panther Ausf. Gs in France. Movement during daylight was dangerous due to constant air raids by Allied fighter-bombers. The turret crew has left the tank. (F. Schulz)

Back from combat near Aachen. This interesting photo shows a Panther Ausf. G of Pz.Rgt. 24 with steel-rimmed running wheels. An O-series was provided with these rubber-saving wheels, probably due to the good experiences the Tiger tanks had with them. This tank also shows a lot of extra equipment. Note how blankets have been hung out to dry from the gun barrel. (E. Bernhardt)

Two Panthers from the same unit, both camouflaged with heavy foliage, meet on a road. The Panther on the left carries an MG 34 in a *Fliegerbeschußgerät* (AA mount), but the ammunition drum is not fitted. The exhaust has been provided with protective covers, and the jack is mounted between the pipes. A towing rope (which would probably be lost soon) has been very slovenly attached to the Panther at right. (F. Schulz)

Another destroyed Panther Ausf. G with steel-rimmed running wheels. This tank probably became a victim of concentrated artillery fire. (E. Bernhardt)

This Panther Ausf. G of Pz.Brig. 106 "Feldherrnhalle " carefully negotiates a corner in the German town of Bonn. The tank, which is of a late production, features the chin gun mantlet. The driver's periscope was provided with an enlarged cover that reduced glare. (BL)

The same Panther seen from behind. Fuel cans are spread over the engine deck, surely not the best place for them. The commander of the tank observes the roads, ready to fire at approaching enemy troops. Combat in cities resulted in heavy losses on both sides. Note the very small number "741" painted in white on the turret. (BL)

Photographed in Berlin in December 1944, this late-model Panther Ausf. G is being used to instruct *Volkssturm* militiamen. The brand new Panther displays no equipment at all, and except for a production number, no markings are evident. The driver's rotating periscope is protected from the sun by a special cover. On the turret is visible the *Nahverteidigungswaffe* , a grenade launcher that was used to fight tank destroyer teams. (BA)

47

This undamaged Panther was abandoned at Tisnov, Czechoslovakia, at the end of April 1945. This is a very late Ausf. G fitted with a flame suppressor exhaust. A lot of extra equipment is carried on the engine deck and the turret. (S. Netrebenko)

This daring *Volkssturm-Mann* places a *Hafthohlladung* magnetic mine onto a Panther's turret. The *Volkssturm* was formed by recruiting children, old men and disabled persons - an obvious sign that the war was lost. The slit cover for the Panther's headlight was removed for this "civil" outing. Of interest is the license plate, which is located near the headlamp. (BA)

Destroyed at Vyskov, Czechoslovakia, another Ausf. G sits abandoned. The gun mantlet is of the late chin type. A lot of extra track links are stored on the turret. Its vehicle number, "215", is painted directly onto the track links. The camouflage scheme, diagonal green and brown stripes, was applied using stencils. (S. Netrebenko)

Destroyed on the Western Front, this Panther Ausf. G is being hauled by a M25 Dragon Wagon. Note how large portions of the *Zimmerit* coating have fallen off. (A. Geibel)

The chin-type gun mantlet prevented shells from being deflected to the thin roof, thus improving the level of ballistic protection. This late Ausf. G was provided with the raised engine cooler on the left side, and its exhaust pipes are fitted with protective covers. The German cross on the turret was non-standard. Overall, Panther "302" seems to be undamaged. (M. Green)

After being hit several times, a battered Panther "126" lies burning on the roadside. Scenes like this were common toward the end of the war when organized counterattacks were the exception to the rule. Hastily established battle groups tried their best to stop the enemy, but were swept away by the same *Blitzkrieg*-type tactics used by the German forces some five years earlier. (A. Geibel)

This brand new Ausf. G of the latest "G" production lot possibly suffered a mechanical breakdown after a short service life. The starter crank can be seen fitted into the rear opening. The camouflage scheme seems to consist of dark yellow and brown over a green base; the running gear is painted completely green. (A. Geibel)

The blast of an internal explosion blew the turret off of this Panther Ausf. G. Of interest is the unusual turret number, "A J 9", the meaning of which is unknown. (S. Netrebenko)

A similar vehicle lies in a heap near a railroad track somewhere in eastern Germany. Note the late-style flame suppressor exhaust tubes. Brackets were welded on both sides of the turret to carry extra road wheels. (S. Netrebenko)

Destroyed or abandoned German tanks were usually collected behind the front line . . . when there was time. This photo shows three Panthers and one Stug IV. (S. Netrebenko)

Panzerbefehlswagen Panther

One of the decisive advantages of German armored warfare was the consequent use of radio equipment. Beginning with the Polish campaign, every armored fighting vehicle (AFV) was provided with a transmitter/receiver to either receive orders or to report observations to higher levels. At the beginning of the war, the German Army had qualitatively good equipment, and the early victories of the *Blitzkrieg* era were gained partly because of the high degree of communication during the battles.

Regimental commanders or ground-to-air liaison officers were provided with the standard transmitter/receiver, and with an additional radio set that was able to operate over greater ranges. With this double radio set, true command tanks were created - a vital condition for the effective leadership of armored formations.

Early *Panzerbefehlswagen* (armored command vehicles) carried a mixture of radio equipment and the highly conspicuous frame antennas. Among these were the Pzbflswg I/A and I/B, the Pzbflswg 35 and 38(t), and the Pzbflswg III. All those early versions had a fixed turret with the main armament deleted, carrying a dummy gun instead to avoid enemy reconnaissance. The first command tank which retained its full capability as a figthing vehicle was the Pzbflswg III Ausf. K. Due to the cramped interior of the turret,

The high degree of communication was one reason for the success of German armored forces. Command tanks like this Pzbflswg III Ausf. B provided the troops with reliable long-distance radio systems. The early command tanks featured dummy guns and highly conspicious frame antennas. (BL)

the 50 mm KWK L/60 was shifted to the left of the mantlet (50 mm KWK 40 *Schmalbewaffnung*).

With the adoption of the Pzkw Panther, and from the beginning of its production, it was decided to create a respective command version of the tank. With the *Befehl* Panthers, a new quality of command tanks appeared. While the radio sets remained unchanged, the assembly, antennas, and other peripheral parts were improved and standardized. In principle, all command tanks built after 1943 had the same radio equipment! The particular sort of radio, however, could change depending on the branch of service; the artillery, for instance, used Fu 16 and Fu 15 radio sets while the tank force had Fu 5 and Fu 8.

When Panther tanks left the factory, between 5 and 10% of them were issued as command tanks (depending on combat losses). At the beginning it was not possible to convert standard MBTs to command tanks in the field. This was changed in July 1944, when an order was issued to equip all tanks with brackets for later fitting of radios and antenna mounts. In theory, it was then possible to replace a disabled Panther command tank by retrofitting a standard fighting tank.

Pzbflswg Panther - Technical Descriptions

Two command tank versions were developed using the Panther tank. The Sd.Kfz. 267, as a standard command vehicle for armored units, and the Sd.Kfz. 268, as a ground-to-air-liasion vehicle.

Pzbflswg Panther Sd. Kfz. 267

The Panther command tank was provided with the standard Fu 5 radio, which was moved into the turret. The 6.5-ft (2-m) rod antenna was fitted on the roof of the turret. An Fu 8 radio set, which was intended for maintaining contact with the baggage train, battalion or regimental staff over long distances (about 43 miles [70

The Pzblfswg III Ausf. K was the first command tank to be provided with a standard tank gun. The 50 mm L/60 was shifted to the left, thus creating space for additional radio equipment in the turret. These vehicles carried a less conspicuous star antenna d instead of the frame antenna. (F. Schulz)

Panther "R 02", the command tank of Standartenführer Mühlenkamp, commander of Pz.Rgt. 5 of 5.SS-Pz.Div. "Wiking", is shown near Kowel during the summer of 1944. Next to it is visible the leader of 8.Company. Mühlenkamp´s vehicle is a Pzbflswg Panther Ausf. A covered with *Zimmerit* . It wears an interesting camouflage scheme of brushed green and brown stripes over dark yellow. The command tank, a Sd.Kfz. 267, is provided with the standard equipment: a 6-foot (2 m) rod antenna on the roof and the star antenna d on the engine deck. (BA)

km]), was mounted in the hull on the transmission. In order to operate, this radio set required a star antenna (1.3-m *Sternantenne d*). This antenna consisted of a basic rod 4 ft (1.3 m) in length upon which six flexible leaf springs were mounted, forming a star shape.

When operating during humid weather, high temperatures could be conducted at the antenna mount. To prevent the rubber of the antenna mounts from melting, the mount was placed into a porcelain isolator. The isolator itself was secured by a short armored tube (*Panzertopf*), which was located at the rear of the engine deck. It was possible to enhance the operating range of Fu 8 radio sets by placing the 1.3-m star antenna on three 4-ft (1.25m)- long elongation tubes. When not in use, these tubes were stored in a rack below the gun cleaning kit. The Panther´s original antenna mount was not used.

Ground-to-air-liaison Vehicle - the Sd.Kfz. 268

The so-called Flivos (*Flieger-Verbindungsoffizier* , or ground-to-air-

liaison officer) contributed much to the early victories of the *Blitzkrieg* era. They coordinated air strikes when they were

needed and warned their own troops when to take cover. Up until 1943, only Pzbflswg III Ausf. Gs were used in the Sd.kfz. 268

This abandoned Pzbflswg Panther Ausf. D, which has slipped off the rail line, features the standard equipment of a Sd.Kfz. 267: the 6-foot (2 m) antenna on top of the turret and the star antenna d in its armored pot located on the engine deck. The tank has also been provided with a ring for the AA MG. (P. Kammann)

role.

Flivo-Panthers featured similar equipment to the Sd.Kfz. 267. Instead of the Fu 8, the Fu 7 radio set was fitted using a 4.5 ft (1.4 m) rod antenna on the standard antenna mount behind the turret. The armored cover for the star antenna remained unused. The exact number of these Flivo-type tanks is unknown. Because the Luftwaffe was busy trying to keep the air over German cities clear, there were hardly any dive-bombers available that could be called off. So it is likely that most of the Sd.Kfz. 268s were used as standard command tanks.

The Panther command tanks performed well in their intended role. Their performance was outstanding, and their instruments were rugged, not being prone to mechanical breakdowns. As Befehlspanthers were hard to identify as command tanks, losses were reduced significantly. Since standard tanks could be reworked at any time (from mid-1944 onwards), command tanks were generally available in sufficient numbers.

Lt. Berger of GD remembers:

"We were satisfied with our Befehlspanthers. Under normal conditions our Fu 5 radio sets had a range of about 5 km [3 miles], more than enough to lead our company's tanks during combat . . . The Fu 8 was used to keep in contact with battalion and regimental staff over long distances. We operated the Fu 8 mainly in the Morse way . . . We had to abandon our command tank two times, and on one occasion we had to rework a standard Panther . . . I never saw this Flivo tank [Sd.Kfz. 268 ground to air liaison vehicle]. Which airplanes should we call? Hermann [Goering] had gambled them all, didn´t he?"

Another Pzbflswg Panther Ausf. A in a French town. Used as an Sd.Kfz. 267 (standard command vehicle for an armored unit) as well, it features the 6-foot (2 m) rod antenna fitted on the turret's roof, but the long-range star antenna d is attached to the standard mount behind the turret. A possible reason for this unusual combination could be that the actual antenna mount was damaged. (F. Schulz)

The same vehicle from behind. The "incorrect" position of the star antenna is evident here. The three elongation tubes for the star antenna, which are normally stored below the gun cleaning kit, are missing. (F.Schulz)

Panther "155", a Pzblfswg Ausf. D, shows off an unusual antenna arrangement, too. Beside the 6-foot (2 m) rod antenna on top of the turret, the star antenna d is fitted onto the usual Panther mount. Since there were only two radio sets, the third antenna in the armored pot is actually superfluous. Below the gun cleaning kit may be seen the elongation tubes for the star antenna. (BA)

A late-model Ausf. D Pzbflswg Panther supervises a railway bridge. This particular tank is interesting because it shows the 6-ft (2-m) rod antenna fitted to the left mount on the hull rather than to the turret's antenna mount, making it clear that any configuration was possible. A lot of extra equipment ws carried on the engine deck. (W. Schneider)

This obscure photo shows a late version of the Pzblfswg Panther Ausf. D belonging to 5.SS-Pz.Div. "Wiking". The commander is reporting the situation to some officers. This vehicle carries a 4.5-ft (1.4 m) rod antenna on the turret, a piece of equipment that is rare. It is possible that this vehicle was used as an SdKfz. 268, the Flivo command tank (ground-to-air communication vehicle). (P. Kammann)

Oberst Willi Langkeit of Pz.Gren.Rgt. "Grossdeutschland" is seen here in the cupola of his Pzbflswg Panther Ausf. A. In front of the vehicle was Oberst Karl Lorenz conferring with his staff officers. Showing the standard antenna equipment, this vehicle was used as a Sd.Kfz. 267. The number "0" indicates its high rank. (BA)

Oberst Willi Langkeit's Panther seen from the left side. Only one of three elongation tubes is still stored in the rack below the gun cleaning kit. General von Manteuffel is seen talking to Oberst Langkeit in his VW Schwimmwagen. (BA)

Oberst Langkeit's tank in combat. This photo was taken during the dramatic tank battle near Targul-Frumos, Romania, where "Grossdeutschland" destroyed more than 250 tanks early in the summer of 1944. (W. Troijca)

A Panther Ausf.G during an inspection. The antenna fitted on the turret of the vehicle indicates that it is probably a command tank. The turret number "I N 3" (meaning unknown) is barely visible; the German cross on the turret is an unsual one. (BL)

This Pzbflswg Panther Ausf. G was demolished at the Western Front. Yet another non-standard Panther, this command tank features three antennas. At least one shell penetrated the turret wall, causing the *Zimmerit* to fall off. The tank also lost one track. (A. Geibel)

Panzerbeobachtungwagen Panther

Pzbeobwg Panther: The Artillery Observer's Vehicle

Beginning in 1943, German tank artillery units were established. Armed with effective self-propelled guns - the 105 mm le.Fh. 18 Wespe and the 150 mm s.Fh. 18 Hummel - they fought alongside the towed regimental and divisional artillery. The fire of the artillery commonly was directed by forward observers who accompanied the line troops. These observers were provided with lightly armored vehicles (Sd.Kfz. 250/6, or something similar), but in most cases they had to ride on combat tanks. This led to criticism as losses were very high. Additionally, this practice was regarded as ineffective because the artillery fire was not directed in the best possible way.

Thus, prior to the Kursk campaign, a number of rebuilt Pzkw IIIs were earmarked for conversion to artillery observer vehicles. The main gun was deleted and replaced by a dummy gun, an observation periscope was mounted on the roof of the turret, and the radio antenna was extended to a degree similar to that of the Pzbflswg III Ausf. K (though it used the same frequency as the artillery radio lines). When the Pzkw IIIs and IVs were retrofitted with armor skirts, the Pzbeobwg IIIs were reworked in a similar way. Consequently, these observer tanks were hardly distinguishable from combat tanks and worked effectively from forward positions.

With the introduction of the Pzkw

When the first German self-propelled artillery units were established, armored artillery observer's vehicles were developed using repaired Pzkw III MBTs. Extended radio equipment was added and the armament was deleted. This photo shows a derelict Pzbeobwg III Ausf. H. The dummy gun, which resembles a 50 mm gun, and the MG ball mount are visible. The *Zimmerit* was added by field workshops. (J. Mueller)

Panther, a new generation of artillery observer´s vehicles was developed. Probably in the summer of 1943, a prototype of the Pzbeobwg Panther was introduced. This prototype, which was built on a late-model Ausf. D, featured a letterbox MG in the hull and pistol ports in the turret sides. The observation devices were much more sophisticated than those of earlier vehicles. The observer, the commander of the tank, had two periscopes

for direct reconnaissance and an integrated observation device. The main gun was replaced by a dummy gun, and the turret´s front plate had two apertures for a stereoscopic rangefinder that was mounted inside.

The author, a Bundeswehr artillery officer of the reserve, will illustrate the everyday activities of a forward observer. When moving up near the MLR with the combat troops, the observer's job is to fullfill the tasks given by the leader of the combat troop, an example of which could be to attack an artillery position. The first

This Pzbeobwg III Ausf. H was heavily converted to be integrated in Pzkw IV units. The original dummy gun was converted with a longer wooden beam and a muzzle brake so the tank would resemble the 75 mm KWK-armed Pzkw IV. *Zimmerit* and a full set of side skirts were added in a field workshop. This photo was taken in Kursk in the summer 1943. (S. Netrebenko)

This is the only photo known to the author that shows the Pzbeobwg Panther. Based on a late-model Ausf. D, the tank's turret was heavily modified. A short dummy gun replaced the L/70 gun. The right flap of the rangefinder that was integrated into the turret front plate is visible beside the machine gun's ball mount. (A. Geibel)

thing he does is determine his own location on a map (this can be rather difficult in the vast steppes of Russia). Proceeding from this position, the observer determines the location of the enemy artillery position. These grid data are then transmitted to the fire mission center, where the data is transformed to direct the fire of the artillery. When the first test shots strike, the observer corrects the fire. As a result, the task is fullfilled by destroying the gun position by firing a minimum of shells. To operate in his own location, the observer needs to know his own location, the observation angle from north to the target, and the range to the target. Experienced artillery officers can work with nothing more than a compass, binoculars and map. Working under such conditions, however, can impair effectiveness and accuracy. An armored observation vehicle offers mobility and protection while this work is accomplished.

The Pzbeobwg Panther offered a variety of instruments. TBF 2 *Turmbeobachtungsfernrohr* was used to find the observer's own location, to determine all needed angles, and to observe the artillery's strikes. The TSR 1 *Sehstab*, mounted in the commander's cupola, allowed the commander to observe from concealed positions. As an alternative, the commander could affix a scissor periscope in the same location. The rangefinder mounted behind the turret's front plate allowed a far more accurate means of finding the range than by the observer's standard method - estimating. Until the introduction of laser rangefinders, this was a common practice in modern armies.

Operating in unknown areas made observing problematic, so a technical device was developed that allowed for the direction of artillery fire without using maps. The exact method of operating the so-called *Blockstelle A* is unknown. However, when working in the proper manner it certainly would have been a breakthrough. The equipment made the Pzbeobwg Panther a most effective observer's vehicle, even when judged by today's standards. Production records state that 41 units were built, probably on repair vehicles. There are, however, no photos known to the author beside the prototype shown in this book.

Bergepanzer Panther

Recovery units depended on the proven Sd. Kfz. 9 heavy half-track and the Sd.Anh. 116 trailer. This combination was sufficient when dealing with Pzkw IIIs or IVs that weighed up to 20 tons. This particular flatbed trailer, which is being towed by a 12-ton half-track, is interesting since it shows a fully closed rear steering cabin. (W. Schneider)

German tank units were provided with integrated recovery and repair units. These company strength units were normally issued at the regimental level (with the exception of heavy tank battalions or independent brigades), and could be called up on demand. The leader would then decide where to send his recovery vehicles.

At the beginning of the war the German tank formations showed a very high standard compared to other nation's forces. During the invasion of France, tank battalions consisted of three light companies (Pzkw I, II and III) and one heavy company (Pzkw IV, some Pzkw II). Every two battalions, which formed a regiment, were provided with a mixed recovery company. The quantity of recovery half-tracks per company varied depending on the respective divison's strength and, of course, combat losses. Normally, ten Sd.Kfz. 7s (8-ton half-tracks) with five Sd.Anh. 115 flatbed trailers (10-ton capacity), and three Sd.Kfz. 9s (18-ton half-tracks) and two Sd.Anh. 116 flatbed trailers (22-ton capacity) belonged to the *Instandsetzungskompanie*.

The situation on the Eastern Front proved to be vastly different from pre-war plans. Here a disabled Stug III Ausf. G is being recovered from muddy terrain. Two 18-ton Famo half-tracks were needed to tow the overloaded Sd. Anh. 116. (H. Hoppe)

Lacking planes, these Luftwaffe troops pose atop a Bergepanther Ausf. D. This versatile recovery vehicle was probably the most important conversion of the Panther. The square steel plates attached to the bow are clearly shown. The crane is dismounted and stored on the right side of the hull. This Panther has received a complete coating of *Zimmerit*. (H. Hoppe)

The *Bergezüge* (recovery platoon) was retained at the train well behind the MLR (main line of resistance). This practice led to criticism since, in emergency situations, the vehicles were too far away for rapid response missions.

This establishment proved to be practical and relatively successful for transporting Pzkw IIIs and IVs, which weighed about 20 tons each. The performance of the towing vehicles was regarded as sufficient. The Famo half-tracks were able to tow disabled tanks from the battlefield under normal conditions. Flatbed trailers could be used to haul over

longer distances. Heavy rain, however, could turn the terrain into muddy swamps. Such situations made recovery difficult and dangerous for both tank and towing vehicle.

The successful course of the early campaigns made the job of the recovery teams quite easy. In most cases, attack operations were successful and retreat was uncommon. So, damaged tanks could be recovered without problems. If the attack got stalled, however, a good situation could easily turn into a bad one. The *Schirrmeister* (motor transport Sgt.) of Inf.Rgt. "Grossdeutschland", Fw. Hoppe,

who is quoted here, was responsible for the temporarily attached Stug Bttr. 640:

"The French artillery defense near Stonne on the 15th of May came as a surprise to 'GD'. After all those lucky engagements, we did not expect such a heavy threat. The assault of the battery, which was relatively weak with only three vehicles, stalled when two Stugs were hit. After our forces were withdrawn, we got the order to immediately recover the slightly damaged No."13", in spite of heavy small arms fire. We drove our Famo as fast as possible backwards to the immobile assault gun. Trees and bushes

The British soldiers seen here can't help but be impressed as they evaluate this Bergepanther, which shows off its rear spade and erected crane. The latter could be mounted on either side of the engine deck. A lot of recovery equipment is visible in this photo. (A. Geibel)

A Bergepanther Ausf. D lies abandoned in a French town. The wooden body was large enough to carry replacement engines or transmissions, which could be fitted using the crane. (J. Mueller)

damage during these actions. A report referring to a recovery of a Tiger Ausf. E over a distance of 93 miles (150 km) [!] resulted in heavy wear to the clutch and transmission of all the half-tracks. The gear box of one Famo had to be entirely exchanged. Furthermore, four precious half-tracks were put out of service for a long time.

The widespread use as towing vehicles of turretless Pzkw IIIs, IVs, or even Vs, and captured enemy tanks was only a short-lived relief. The lack of spare parts and the overall bad state of these old vehicles quickly put an end to their careers.

Along with the development of the Panther, the creation of a respective recovery version was planned. Though MAN had promised production of 308 Panther MBT´s by May 1943, the number of completed tanks did not exceed 100 units. The critical situation in which the heavily pressed manufacturer was in made the immediate delivery of the so-called *Bergepanther* impossible. Aware of this, MAN was ordered to produce 12 turretless Panthers as stop-gap recovery tanks, which were called *Bergewannen*. These were delivered in early June 1943. The firm of Henschel proceeded to work on the *Bergepanther* then, and during the period between July and October, 70 units were delivered. The *Bergepanther* was provided with a powerful 40-ton winch in the lower superstructure, which was driven by the

concealed this operation, and the silent-running engine helped us to approach unnoticed, but the last fifty meters [165 feet] had to be covered without any camouflage. Luckily we were fast, and the wireless operator of the Stug fastened the towing ropes. The recovery finally succeeded with only one man getting slightly wounded."

This report shows that recovery teams lived a dangerous life. But it showed, too, that the initial establishment was reliable and adequate. The introduction of the new heavy tanks in 1943 would bring more serious problems to the *Bergezüge*. Due to combat losses and missing production capacities, the fixed number of 13 half-tracks per engineer company was seldom reached. Since Panther and Tiger units were regarded as most important, quite often neighboring units had to give up their precious recovery vehicles. Anyway, 1943 meant a turning point in every respect. Not only were the Famos not available in sufficient numbers (in fact there were never enough until the end of hostilities), the increased weight of the new tanks meant that the flatbed trailers couldn´t be used anymore. Direct recovery from the battlefield was practically impossible as the Famos were too weak. What is worse, the Panthers and Tigers were more prone to mechanical breakdowns than the Pzkw IIIs and IVs, thus doubling the problems. Recovery of Panthers by other Panther tanks was forbidden because there was a danger of a breakdown of the transmission and clutch of another tank . Nevertheless, this practice was quite common. Obergefreiter Lenz of Pz.Rgt. 4 recalls:

"We [the crews of the Panther tanks, author] were instructed not to use our tanks for recovery actions. We faced heavy disciplinary punishment when our tank would break down, too . . . Of course, we helped our comrades whenever it was necessary."

The harsh reality of the fighting at the Eastern Front demanded that, depending on the ground, up to four Famos had to be used to recover a Panther tank, and up to five for a Tiger Ausf. E (source: H. Maus). The half-tracks used suffered heavy

This photo shows the result of an Allied air strike that surprised a unit while it was crossing a bridge. The Bergepanther is totally destroyed, providing us a view into the engine and winch compartment. (J. Mueller)

Panther´s turret traverse system. The towing cable passed over the engine deck. A large rear spade was attached at the rear plate. A standard recovery situation saw the *Bergepanther* towing a disabled tank from the battlefield using a V-shaped towing device. In case a direct recovery was not possible (because of heavy mud, for example), the *Bergepanther* approached the damaged tank and lowered the rear spade with the winch cable. When connected, the winch would be operated, forcing the spade into the ground and moving the disabled tank. After covering a certain distance, the *Bergepanther* would disconnect the winch, drive, and move on, leaving the disabled tank behind, with the spade gliding over the surface. Then the procedure was repeated. The winch worked well, and its capacity could be doubled using a pulley. Two square plates were attached at the bow to hold a wooden beam when the *Bergepanther* had to push disabled vehicles.

A variety of other special tools were carried with the vehicle. A two-ton crane could be erected behind the winch compartment. Using this crane, engines and transmissions could be lifted and exchanged. The deck above the winch was reinforced to carry spare units. Fuel capacity was extended to 284 gallons (1,075 liters) [compared to 1,900 gallons (7,201 liters) for the Panther MBT]. Support brackets at the glacis plate allowed

This dramatic shot shows a failed attempt to recover a disabled Tiger Ausf. E. The armored Bergepanther was able to move up to the Tiger and connect its towing device. Apparently, though, before it could start the recovery, it also took a hit. (S. Netrebenko)

the fitting of a 20 mm KWK 38 machine gun for self-defense. It appears, however, that this weapon was not used too often. For this reason the gun mount was deleted beginning with the production of the Ausf. G. The shape of the rear spade was changed several times, probably according to combat reports. Approximately 350

Bergepanthers were produced up to the end of war.

The *Bergepanther* was issued to the troops in considerable quantities from July 1943 onward. It was planned that each Panther battalion would be provided with a recovery/maintenance company equipped with two *Bergepanthers* and thirteen Famos. Although it seems this schedule was fulfilled, the troops demanded more *Bergepanthers*. Four of these useful vehicles were desired for each battalion.

Summarizing, then, the *Bergepanther* was an excellent recovery vehicle. Under standard conditions, its performance was sufficient to tow damaged vehicles directly from the battlefield, and the powerful winch allowed the recovery of heavy tanks from wet terrain. A veteran remembers:

"I was detached from a Stug-Brigade to GD (Pz.Gren.Div. Grossdeutschland) . . . The change from my old Famo to the Bergepanther was incredible. We could always help, even under enemy fire. I can recall a situation when a comrade was hit by 7.62 cm fire during a recovery. The shell bounced off the front plate, and the vehicle still rescued a disabled Panther. There were no casualties . . . On the other hand, we had severe problems with the final drives [as all Panthers had in early 1944, author]. We carried spare parts for the transmission wherever there was free space."

Another abandoned Bergepanther somewhere in France. Like most of these vehicles that we've seen, this is an Ausf. D. Both the driver's sight flap and the MG port are opened. Large portions of the *Zimmerit* coating have fallen off, possibly due to small arms fire. The wooden body is missing, and some extra roadwheels are visible on the metal superstructure. The 2 cm KWK mount was not fitted. (K. Münch)

Panther Crew

Carefully looking out of his cupola, this Panther commander wears a *Schiffchen* field cap with headphones. He holds a signal pistol in his hand, possibly indicating that combat would start soon. This Panther even wears a coating of *Zimmerit* around the cupola. The bent metal strip in the cupola is where the platform for the IR set would be located. (P. Kammann)

Wearing only grey tricot shirts, officers belonging to "Wiking" have a chat atop a Panther. The commander is wearing his Knight's Cross, which normally was worn on the uniform only on the day it was awarded. The *Zimmerit's* appearance is clearly seen here. (P. Kammann)

This "Wiking" tank crew wears a combination of the standard black trousers and the camouflaged uniform jacket. All have the black *Schiffchen* field caps. (P. Kammann)

Dressed in black tanker's trousers and tricot shirts, these crew members pose in front of a Panther that is adorned with a three-color camouflage scheme. (P. Kammann)

Two men of "Wiking" are seen here, the one on the left wearing only a standard uniform jacket over his tank overall, and the other sporting only overalls. The tank in the background, a Panther Ausf. A, shows a very rough *Zimmerit* coating. The MG port is closed off with a plug plate. (P. Kammann)

Lieutenant Finsterwalder of Panzer-Lehr Regiment 130 is seen wearing a motorcycle coat over his black uniform. His field cap is black as well. (F. Schulz)

A lieutenant of Panzer-Lehr Regiment 130 discusses the situation with some Panzergrenadiers in June 1944 outside Villers Bocage. (F. Schulz)

Three tankers on top of their Panther. All wear the standard tanker trousers and field shirts. (P. Kammann)

Wearing his 1943-style camouflage overalls, this officer strikes a pose standing in the cupola of his Panther. He had only been awarded the Knight´s Cross recently. (P. Kammann)

"Sperber", "Biwa" & "Uhu"

In the early '30s work began on a most remarkable technology that lead to the first night-observation devices. After long and inconceivable delays, the German military used the results of this work on the battlefields. The author based this chapter on a number of sources. Important facts were provided by an article published in the March 1957 issue of the monthly magazine "Der deutsche Soldat". Mr. Erwin Bernhardt, former *Panzerwart* (tank mechanic) of 1.Abt./Pz.Rgt. 24, contributed the precious memories of an eyewitness. An obscure photo, provided by Mr. Franz Schmidt, unveiled further details that were until now unknown. Last but not least, the book Der Krieg in der Heimat, a compilation of the events that occured around the German town of Uelzen during the last months of WW II, provided valuable hints about combat engagements in which infrared equipment was used.

IR night-vision equipment was tested on many different vehicles. This Marder II, wearing the number "S 12", shows an IR search light/image converter combination on top of the Pak 40. Another image converter was added to the left of the driver's side visor. (F. Schmidt)

The roots of infrared fighting capabilities go back to the late 1930s. The firm of AEG introduced the so-called "Braunsche Röhre" (cathode ray tube) in 1934. This was the essential part needed to construct an image converter that could transform infrared light into perceptible light. As early as 1939 AEG offered a military version of this infrared light/image converter set; it was introduced with a 37

mm Pak 36 to the Army High Command. Although the set was in the prototype state; it was bulky and very prone to mechanical breakdowns. It showed one fact clearly: it is possible to fight enemy vehicles at night (at specific ranges)! The HWA (Army Ordnance Bureau) supervised the tests and

set a basic requirement that any nighttime aiming device used with a gun (for instance the 37 mm Pak) "should offer the same hit probability as achieved when firing the gun in daylight". Of course this was impossible, and further tests were drastically limited . . . and any support to this young, highly sophisticated technology was rejected.

In the autumn of 1942, however, the infrared aiming device was tested again on a 75 mm Pak 40, and now the standards were set lower. Apparently, the tests were concluded successfully in mid-1943, and production of these devices was ordered for different purposes. When in the spring of 1944 about 1,000 IR aiming devices were delivered, army officials again rejected their use. The ready and working devices were stored in a salt mine in the Harz mountains. A general of the general staff was quoted as saying, "We don't need any stuff like this, our soldiers will win the war chivalrously".

The change in warfare after the D-Day invasion of 6 June 1944 caused a dramatic increase in losses at the new Western Front (for example, US dive bombers reported the destruction of about 400 German tanks between the 25th and 31st of July 1944). Thus, safe movement was possible only at night. Now that IR sets were needed for survival, a supply was quickly ordered.

Only a few months later, IR devices were introduced in limited numbers to the Army and the Luftwaffe. The section

This obscure photo shows a Panther Ausf. D fitted with a triple IR search light/image converter set. 1) This is the commander's IR set, which is coupled with an MG 34. 2) The gunner had an image converter fitted in front of one of his two monocular gun sights. 3) Finally, the driver had an image converter fitted to his open sight flap. Similarly modified vehicles were reworked towards the end of the war and were apparently used in combat. Note the Willys Jeep in the background. (F. Schmidt)

entitled "Technical Groundwork" will explain the technical principle; the sections "Vehicles Used with IR Devices" and "The IR Panthers" will explain the use of this technology by the Wehrmacht.

Technical Groundwork of IR Night-Viewing Devices

The German IR technology of WW II was based on the fact that infrared light is reflected in a manner very similar to normal daylight, and that these reflected infrared beams can be converted into perceptible light. Basically, two instruments were used: a searchlight with a filter that emitted infrared light and an image converter able to convert the IR light into perceptible light. Both devices could vary as to size and performance depending on different applications.

The infrared light would be reflected from a target back into the converter tube in which a "Braunsche Röhre" - cathode ray tube - functioned to convert the light. The converter tube featured a strong visor with a windshield at the front to offer protection. It was possible to add optics to the converter to meet any particular specification, depending on the use to which the converter was put. The converter worked with a potential up to 17,000 V. Power was provided by an HS 5F high-voltage transformer. One tranformer could supply high voltage to a number of different converters, the output being much greater than that acquired under ordinary operating conditions.

German Designations for IR Devices

The different IR search lights, which varied in size and performance, were all called "Infrarot-Scheinwerfer", with the diameter of the light preceeding the name (e.g. *20 cm Scheinwerfer*). All IR searchlights received the descriptive designation "*Uhu*", for "owl".

The converter tube was called *Bildwandler*. This designation was abbreviated to *Biwa* (*Bildwandler*). According to their use, the IR sets received specific designations. The Wehrmacht used three aiming devices: *Zielgerät* 1128, 1221 and 1222; three night-driving devices: "*Fahrgerät* 1250, 1252 and 1253; and an observation device: "*Beobachtungsgerät* " 1251.

This list is not complete as much remains unknown about this equipment today.

Vehicles Used with IR Sets

As stated above, the first gun fitted with an IR set (IR search light and converter) was the 37 mm Pak 36. No further details are available. A number of the standard antitank guns (the 75 mm Pak 40, for example) were fitted with IR sets (a 30 cm search light and a *Zielgerät* 1221) from 1944 onward. Trucks could be fitted with a 30 cm IR search light and the *Fahrgerät* 1253 driving device. A Marder II (75 mm Pak 40) was fitted with a 30 cm search light and the *Zielgerät* 1221 on the superstructure, and with a *Fahrgerät* 1253 driving device, which was mounted inside the vehicle in front of the driver. Mounting was lateral, and the driver could see through the left side visor using the *Fahrgerät* as a lateral periscope.

Apparently, a Jagdpanther unit received a number of IR sets similar to the simple equipment fitted on some Panther Gs.

Since the IR technology was available at the end of 1944, it is possible that more tests were performed using many different vehicles. Clear combat reports, however, are known only for the Panther MBTs and the accompanying Sd.Kfz. 251 APCs.

IR Aiming, Driving, and Observation Devices on the Panther MBT

The first tests of these devices were started in late 1943. Standard production Panthers were sent to Fallingbostel to the *Panzertruppenschule* (armor school). Here, apparently, two different solutions were developed and used in combat.

Solution A - *Sperber* (sparrow hawk): The IR set for Solution A consisted of one IR searchlight and one image converter. Inside the commander´s cupola a tiny table was mounted, which was fixed in the 12 o'clock position. The table served as a platform for one 30 cm IR searchlight (200 W) and one image converter. Inside the tank there were a number of additional instruments. A second 12 V battery supplied power to a transformer, which transformed the voltage to 17,000 V. As the battery could supply this for only about 4 hours, it was charged by a generator.

The commander used this IR set to direct the driver, who could see nothing at night. This driving required a good deal of training time, which was not available toward the end of the war. Additionally, the commander searched targets with his converter. When a target was detected, the commander gave the order to the gunner, either spoken or by body contact (a touch by a hand or a foot on the left shoulder

would mean "turn left"), to move the turret. When the target appeared again in the converter´s sight, the platform was fixed in the 12 o'clock position. Then the commander determined the range and, when he was sure of it, gave the order to fire. This was a primitive style of target designation.

The effective range of this IR set was about 546 to 655 yards (500 to 600 m). This, unfortunately, limited the use of the formidable L/70 gun. For this reason, larger search lights were mounted on Sd. Kfz. 251 APCs (the 60 cm AA search light was altered to emit IR beams). These APCs had converters as well. When targets were detected, their location would be transmitted via the Fu 5 radio set to the Panther tanks of the unit, which would take over. The guns were fired using flash-proof ammunition to minimize the chance of detection by the target [source: 'Der deutsche Soldat', March 1957].

The *3.Schwadron* (squadron) of 1./Pz.Rgt. 24 (attached to 116.Tank Division until 25 November 1944) was sent to armor school in Bergen, which was located near Fallingbostel. This company was fitted with IR devices of Solution A [source: E. Bernhardt]. Other sources refer to this solution as *Sperber* (sparrow hawk). The author of the essay in 'Der deutsche Soldat' magazine stated that a trained crew could fight targets at up to 2,733 yards (2,500 m). He reported that two of every three shots were hits. [This sounds overly optimistic in the author´s opinion]. Later, a special arrangement was tested, which indicated to the gunner all of the vertical movements of the commander's. Additionally, it was planned that the driver´s periscope would be exchanged for a vertically installed IR converter that would provide night vision.

In early 1945 one Panther that had been fitted with a *Sperber* set was ordered to the front at Stuhlweissenburg in Hungary. It was most probably accompanied by a Sd.Kfz. 251 fitted with a 60 cm "Uhu" IR searchlight and an Sd. Kfz. 251 "Falke" support vehicle. It is reported that the *Sperber* combination worked very successfully.

The whole battalion, including 3rd Squadron - with at least 17 Panthers that were initially thus equipped - was sent to Hungary **without** the IR sets in early 1945. Mr. Bernhardt remembers that all IR devices had to be left in Fallingbostel before his unit was entrained at Bergen. No reason has been found for this order.

This crippled Panther lay near the town of Uelzen for a long time before it was fully scrapped. This early Ausf. D still shows two welding marks on the mantlet below the gun sight. It is possible that this vehicle was provided with a triple IR set of Solution B. (F. Schulz)

Another photo of the same tank taken in 1946. The Panther has been totally stripped, probably by local farmers and scrap dealers. Note the welding marks below the gun sight. (F. Schulz)

In early 1945, *Panzerdivision* "Clausewitz" saw combat in the Fallersleben area; it had orders to fight its way south to the Harz mountains. Although organised as a *Panzerdivison*, the unit had very little armor. Two of its Panther tanks were reportedly equipped with IR devices (probably the *Sperber*). One bit of action took place on the 21st of April 1945. The last ten tanks of "Clausewitz", followed by a Sd.Kfz. 234/1 recce vehicle, approached a US antitank gun position (76 mm AT gun M2) at the Weser/Elbe Canal. The first attack took place at two o'clock in the morning. The Americans were alert and fired illumination rounds. The leading Panther was hit and slipped into a ditch, and the attack was halted. Then the IR Panthers took cover. After a short time they located the guns and fired some twenty rounds. The entire position was destroyed, and the gun crews and the accompanying infantry company escaped in somewhat of a panic. The IR Panthers followed up, destroying some trucks and other support vehicles.

The attack was a success, revealing the enormous possibilities of IR technology. It is not known whether the *Sperber*-Panthers of "Clausewitz" were used a second time.

In March 1945 *Panzerdivison* "Müncheberg" was established. Famous author Tony Le Tessier states in his book Duchbruch an der Oder that the tank battalion was equipped with 11 Pzkw IVs (1st Co.), 10 Pzkw Vs (2nd Co.) and 10 Pzkw IVs (3rd Co.). Second Company apparently was provided with a number of *Sperber* devices.

IR solution "A" was a very simple way to enable tanks to fight at night. The *Sperber* set was very versatile; it could be easily mounted on almost every military vehicle. It was possible to fight enemy vehicles at night over short to medium ranges. One disadvantage was that the commander had to direct the driver and the gunner along with commanding the tank. What is more, the whole technology was prone to mechanical damage, with the cathode ray tubes being particularly vulnerable.

Solution A could be fitted to all production lots of the Panther. A recently recovered Panther Ausf.G in Poland shows welded brackets on the cover of the driver's frontal periscope. Since the driver's seat on late Panthers could be elevated, it might be possible that an image converter was fitted directly in front of the driver's hatch, thus enabling the driver to see during night.

Solution B: Apparently there was another as yet unknown version of IR Panther built towards the end of the war. As Fallingbostel had a large number of *Biwa* sets in stock, it is possible that these were used for "sophisticated improvisations" when Allied forces approached. The author can present a photo of such a type, which was taken by British or US troops, judging by the uniforms and the Willys Jeep.

While Solution A was a simple addition of an IR light/image converter, which could be fitted to almost every vehicle, Solution B was much more elaborate.

The greatest disadvantage of Solution A was that it offered IR night viewing cabability only to the commander. The layout of the Panther Ausf. G and the later Ausf. As, however, did not allow for providing the gunner with image converters without greater changes to the basic MBT's design. So an intermediate solution was sought and finally found. Older model Panthers (Ausf. D and early Ausf. A), being reworked in German factories, were chosen for a most interesting modification. As these vehicles had a large moveable visor flap in the front armor for the driver, it was easy to add an image converter here. When using the converter, the visor was opened and the armored glass was removed. The converter could be fixed upon a tiny mount, which was welded to the frontal armor plate directly under the visor. A 30 cm IR light was fitted to the right of the visor.

Both Panther Ausf. Ds and the early Ausf. A were fitted with the binocular telescopic sight, while later versions had a monocular one. In the case of the binocular sight, a technical improvisation was possible: the binocular sight could be replaced by two monocular telescopes. In daylight the gunner would use the left monocular for aiming; at night he would use the right one, which had a converter in front of its frontal aperture. To the left of the periscopes was mounted the 30 cm IR searchlight. The whole arrangement was fitted on a tiny table, which was welded to the mantlet below the two periscope apertures. The commander had an improved IR device, which was used with the Sd. Kfz. 251/21 "Falke ". This was a parallel mount comprising a 30 cm IR search light, the image converter and a MG 34 or 42. On the Panther, however, The MG 34 was used, since its bow and turret MGs were this model; the supply of spare parts could be rationed this way.

To minimize the danger of detection, all Solution B-type IR Panthers were equipped with the flame-proof tubular exhausts used on late Ausf. G Panthers. Also, there was an order to destroy all IR devices after the loss of a tank.

Mr. Bernhardt of Pz.Rgt. 24 remembers:

"All IR sets were secured to stick hand grenades. Strings led from the opened bottom screws [of the grenades] to the commander. When he left the disabled tank, as last man of his crew to leave, he would ignite the grenade by pulling the strings."

This probably was a stop-gap solution born in the last weeks of a lost war. The Wehrmacht had demolition charges for such purposes.

It is very likely that these heavily modified IR Panthers saw action towards the end of the war. The first evidence of this is the photo shown in this chapter, which depicts a Panther tank fitted with three IR devices.

Some reports tell of late-war combat involving IR Panthers that were so equipped, which encountered a British armored divison. A British unit equipped with Comet tanks was engaged in April 1945 (at night) by some Solution B-type IR Panthers. In a short, fierce, one-sided firefight, the entire platoon was annihilated. Two further photos appearing in this chapter, which were taken in 1947, show a Panther Ausf. D. These photos show more or less clearly some welding marks at the gun's mantlet. That is where the tiny table for the gunner's IR arrangement was fitted. Possibly it was removed by the British for testing purposes after the end of the war.

With this sophisticated technique in mind, some farsighted officers of the Fallingbostel armor school formed basic tactics for equipped tank units. They planned to establish special night task forces. Panthers fitted with triple IR devices formed the core of these units. These tanks had three huge armor plates welded on the engine deck, thus offering protection on the sides and rear for three infantrymen. These troops had to protect "their" Panther with MP 44 assault rifles, which could be fitted with IR devices in its final version.[*Vampir*].

The IR Panther would be followed into combat by Sd.Kfz. 251/21 "*Falke*" vehicles carrying a number of infantrymen armed with MP 44s. The attack would have been backed, whenever possible, by Sd.Kfz. 251/20s fitted with 60 cm "*Uhu*" IR search lights. Units that were equipped in this manner would surely have had an enormous impact on enemy units that lacked IR devices.

Ersatz M10

This is one of Pz.Brig. 150's Ersatz M10s. About ten Panther Ausf. Gs were carefully concealed with metal sheets to resemble the US tank destroyer M10. A shell crushed the M10-style lining on the gun mantlet, but failed to penetrate. The vehicles were camouflaged in olive drab and were provided with US-style markings. (S. Zaloga)

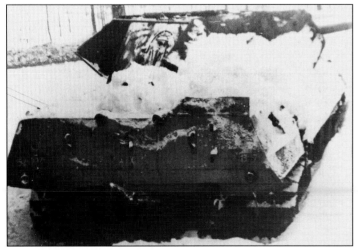

The same vehicle from the rear. Even the rear plate has been thoroughly concealed, making it almost impossible to recognize the shape of the Panther. Note that even small details like loops and cat's eyes were reproduced. (S. Zaloga)

The top view shows that even the commander's hatch of the Panther was removed for this modification. This particular Panther was a late-model Ausf. G command tank, as is evident by the mounts for the auxiliary crane and the antenna mount on the left of the split hatch. Note how the false side plates were attached. (S. Zaloga)

The shape of the Panther in this photo has been effectively concealed. (S. Zaloga)

Spring 1945. This fake M10 was destroyed in a town in Luxembourg. The hatch in front of the bow MG has fallen off. (J. Mueller)

With its turret pointing to the rear, this Ersatz M10 drove into a house before being abandoned. Sections of spare tracks were attached to the hull sides to make the vehicle further resemble the M10. Note the US-style star that was sprayed onto the turret. (J. Mueller)

This Ersatz M10 was hit several times. The thin sheet metal has been partially ripped off by the impact of fire. (J. Mueller)

A G.I. stands in front of a fourth destroyed Ersatz M10, his right foot on the torn away turret lining. (J. Mueller)

Pz.Brig. 150 used ten Ersatz M10s, a number of Sd.Kfz. 251s and some strange Stug IIIs. These were converted as well, with new side skirts being added to cover the entire running gear. The disguised tank was sprayed olive green and received US-style markings. This destroyed vehicle even lacks the muzzle brake. (J. Mueller)

G.I.s inspect another concealed Stug III. This was a late-production vehicle, as the cast mantlet and the return rollers indicate. Pz.Brig. 150 conducted a number of unsuccessful assaults due to incorrect combat tactics. (J. Mueller)

Panther pill-box

During the fighting in Italy, the Germans prepared a defensive line south of Rome. Since the Allied advance could be slowed down, there was enough time to establish fortifications and pillboxes. The *Goten-Linie* was reinforced by Panther turrets, which would supervise crucial positions with their effective guns. This particular pillbox was totally destroyed, the Ausf. D turret having been blown off its mount. (A. Geibel)

To defend the eastern borders, many German cities were declared to be *feste Plätze* - improvised fortresses. All effort was undertaken to reinforce these defensive lines. Many tank turrets, and even completely damaged tanks, were partially buried. This photo shows the turret of a ruined Panther covered by debris. (S. Netrebenko)

This Ausf. D turret was placed in the middle of the street. Positions like this normally could not be held, since the turrets could be easily bypassed. Note that even the commander's cupola was removed. (S. Netrebenko)

Berlin children play on a dug-in Panther. This Ausf. G was probably destroyed on the Eastern Front and then sent back to Germany where it was used to defend the capital. Note that the turret shows a point of penetration, which was welded shut with a rectangular plate. (H. Hoppe)

Another Panther that has dug-in at an unknown German city. This Ausf. G lacks complete running gear. Its turret has been penetrated by at least four shells. (S. Netrebenko)

Soviet Panther

An unknown number of captured German tanks were repaired by the Soviets. Apparently several units were entirely equipped with Panther tanks. (S. Netrebenko)

Soviet tankers pose on three Panther Ausf. A tanks. The vehicles appear to be in a perfect shape. They received a new dark green overspray and large white stars. Many captured German tank mechanics were pressed into service with these units. (S. Netrebenko)

Jagdpanther

Beside the Bergepanther recovery tank, the Jagdpanther was the most important derivative of the Panther MBT. This early version (so identified by the narrow bulge around the gun assembly), which is part of 3./s.Pzjg.Abt. 654 at Bourgtheroulde, is towing another disabled tank destroyer. The crew apparently confiscated some umbrellas for their personal use. Compare the hull's shape with that of the Panther Ausf.G and A. (K. Münch)

The Jagdpanther was a highly feared opponent. Armed with the 88 mm Pak 43/3, it could destroy any enemy tank at distances well beyond 3,280 yards (3,000 m). This particular vehicle is from a later production lot. In 1944 the base color of some German AFV was changed to dark green, then camouflage of dark yellow and brown was applied. This scheme was more effective in the greener vegetation of middle Europe. The Jagdpanther is standing in front of some Pz IV/70(V)s at an enemy vehicle assembly location. (M. Green)